The
INDEPENDENCE

NATIONS

David Fromkin

THE
INDEPENDENCE
OF
NATIONS

THE
INDEPENDENCE
OF
NATIONS

David Fromkin

PRAEGER

Westport, Connecticut
London

Library of Congress Cataloging in Publication Data

Fromkin, David.
  The independence of nations.

  Includes index.
  1. International relations.   I. Title.
JX1391.F76   327.1   81-12093
ISBN 0-275-91697-9
ISBN 0-275-91509-3 (pbk.)

Library of Congress Catalog Card Number: 81-12093
ISBN: 0-275-91509-3

First published in 1981

Praeger Publishers, 88 Post Road West, Westport, CT 06881
An imprint of Greenwood Publishing Group, Inc.

Printed in the United States of America

The paper used in this book complies with the Permanent
Paper Standard issued by the National Information Standards
Organization (Z39.48-1984).

16 15 14

To GRACE DARLING

whose name says it all

CONTENTS

INTRODUCTION

This is a book about why world politics are what they are. I
began to write it in 1979, on the occasion of an anniversary: it
was forty years since the appearance of a book about international
relations that caused a greater stir than anything published before
or since. I used that book as at once my model and my adversary. It
was E. H. Carr's *The Twenty Years' Crisis;* and it challenged the
idealistic democratic world to develop a science of international
relations that would give due importance to the realities of power.
It was an inspiring and provoking book. It is worth reconsidering
for its own sake, and also because the issues that it raised are still
the subject of debate and disagreement.

Remarkable though it may seem, it is only in the last few
decades that international relations has been recognized as an
academic field of its own, so that courses in it are offered as such in
schools and universities. The recognition came with the publication of Carr's book in 1939, of Frederick L. Schuman's textbook in
1933, and of Hans Morgenthau's *Politics Among Nations* in 1948.[1]

---

[1]Frederick L. Schuman, *International Politics: An Introduction to the
Western State System* (New York and London: McGraw Hill Book Company,
1933); E. H. Carr, *The Twenty Years' Crisis, 1919-1939: An Introduction to the
Study of International Relations* (London: Macmillan and Co., 1939); Hans J.

In historical terms, the 1930s and 1940s, when these books appeared, were not more than a moment ago, so that, as E. H. Carr wrote in the first sentence of his book: "The science of international politics is in its infancy."[2]

Not even governments, until the recent past, felt obliged to inquire into the affairs of parts of the world remote from the concerns of their own countries. It is only recently, too, that the Council on Foreign Relations in New York and the Royal Institute of International Affairs in London were founded: in 1919 leading English and American delegates to the Peace Conference decided that such institutions ought to be created when they discovered that most of the delegates knew little about the intricacies of the political affairs of the world whose fate they had met to determine.[3]

It is surprising. International relations have overshadowed private lives and concerns since the beginning of time and have turned human beings into pawns on the chessboards of public destinies. The exigencies of national ambitions and rivalries have taken the lives of many and affected the lives of everyone. History's headlines have been about war and peace; and from the very beginning, people ought to have wondered what it was all about.

Since the end of the 1914 war, a start has been made, but the question remains as to why it took so long — why indeed we know so little about international relations even now. A visitor from the far side of the sky, on being told that we have, at best, only an imperfect idea of how our own political entities act and interact, might well conclude that the human race has no curiosity about

---

Morgenthau, *Politics Among Nations: The Struggle for Power and Peace* (New York: Alfred A. Knopf, 1948).

[2]Carr, *Crisis,* p. 3. This does not mean that it cannot draw upon classics in other fields. The works of historians such as Thucydides and Guicciardini, of philosophers such as Hobbes and Kant, of political analysts such as Machiavelli and memorialists such as the Cardinal de Retz, and of international law theorists such as Grotius and Vattel are among those to which writers about international relations often refer.

[3]*The Council on Foreign Relations: A Record of Twenty-Five Years, 1921–1946* (New York: January 1, 1947).

itself and about the possibility that it might change its institutions for the better and thus save itself from the terrible fates with which it is threatened.

Many attempts have been made to explain this apparent lack of curiosity. Perhaps the correct explanation is the simplest one: that the truth about international relations is disagreeable, and that it is usual and normal to not want to think about things that are disagreeable.

Strains of this disposition to ignore whatever is disagreeable also are characteristic of much of what *is* written and said about world affairs. Hence the professed belief that the national state is a thing of the past, and that what is most significant in the contemporary world is the increase in cooperative ventures between nations. There indeed has been such an increase, which is welcome news; but also there has been an increase in conflict and an increase in everything else, so that whether the *proportion* of international behavior that is cooperative has risen or fallen is at least open to question.

Ever since the conclusion of the International Telegraph Union in the 1860s and the Universal Postal Union in the 1870s, optimists also have claimed that a web of international technical and economic agencies would bring about a cooperative world order, but as yet it has not done so; nor have ambitious peace-keeping schemes, such as the League of Nations and the United Nations, done so. That is not to deny the importance of the tremendous strides forward made by these agencies in their own fields; it is merely to point out that they have not brought about a peaceful world order.

There have been important changes, certainly, but for better or for worse, what continues to be fundamental in international relations is the independence of states. The most significant change is that it continues to be fundamental now that monarchies, dynastic empires, and other older types of states have given way to the national state, with the result that independence has been enlisted in the service of nationalism. It is that change which poses questions of especial difficulty for the world of today — questions with which I shall try to deal in the pages that follow. The title, by referring to nations rather than to states, is intended to frame the time and the issues with which the book is primarily concerned. I have chosen it, not to blur the difference between states and nations, but to emphasize it.

"Nations," as a word that evokes emotion, also suggests what I shall attempt to show in the last chapter: that the fragmentation of the political world is neither accidental nor arbitrary, but rather results from rooted patterns of human behavior.

The road to the last chapter is a relatively straightforward one, but perhaps it may be even easier to follow if I outline it briefly in advance. In Chapter 1, I describe the search for a peaceful world that began in the aftermath of the First World War and continues today. The search was and is conducted by scholars seeking to explain the nature of international relations; and in Chapter 2, I suggest that their method of studying it has affected their conclusions and therefore ours. In particular, I write that they have ignored such special characteristics as the independence (Chapter 2) and the corporate character (Chapter 3) of states. This leads them (I argue in Chapter 4) to write about events that do not occur significantly in international affairs, such as arbitrations and adjudications, rather than important events such as partitions and the flight of refugees, which occur all the time. In Chapter 5, I write that this same error — the failure to recognize the special characteristics of international affairs — leads governments and peoples alike to choose foreign policies that produce results the very opposite of those intended. The most important example, which is provided in Chapter 6, results from the search for justice and peace in a world structured in such a way that the one can be had only at the expense of the other. It is that kind of world because it is politically disunited; and, as shown in Chapter 7, it is of divided heart as well, because there are strong impulses towards unity that are overcome only by the stronger pull of diverse politics. How to evaluate the competing claims of unity and diver-

sity was a matter on which opinion in the nineteenth century tended to differ from our own; the merits of the two points of view are
compared in Chapter 8.

How to repair the fundamental flaw in the way in which we
think and act in international relations is the subject of the concluding chapter and brings us back to the book's starting point: the
determination of the generation of 1914 to launch us on a journey
toward a world of justice and peace. The question now, as then, is
of the direction which that journey ought to take.

THE
INDEPENDENCE
OF
NATIONS

1

NO MAN'S LAND

In 1914, citizens of the United States and of the Western European countries enjoyed freedom and physical security to an extent hardly conceivable today. George Kennan writes that Americans at that time "had a sense of security vis-à-vis their world environment such as I suppose no people had ever had since the days of the Roman Empire."[1] There had been no major war for a long time. Governments, foreign and domestic, left one alone. In his *English History*, A. J. P. Taylor says that "Until 1914 a sensible, law-abiding Englishman could pass through life and hardly notice the existence of the state, beyond the post office and the policeman. He could live where he liked and as he liked. He had no official number or identity card. He could travel abroad or leave his country for ever without a passport or any sort of official permission."[2] He also could stay at home, and not worry that foreigners would invade it.

---

[1] George F. Kennan, *American Diplomacy: 1900–1950* (Chicago and London: The University of Chicago Press, 1951), p. 3.

[2] A. J. P. Taylor, *English History: 1914–1945* (Oxford: At the Clarendon Press, 1965), p. 1.

In that world without passports, the summer of 1914 was felt to be, of all moments, the most idyllic. It was, in the words of a French novelist, "Le plus bel été du monde"—the most beautiful summer in the world.[3] A recent historian describes it as "warm and sunny, eminently pastoral. One lolled outside on a folding canvas chaise, or swam, or walked in the countryside. One read outdoors, went on picnics, had tea served from a white wicker table under the trees."[4] From the English countryside, a few days before summer began, the young poet Rupert Brooke wrote that "The last few days here have been glorious, and the air is so heavy (but not sleepy) with the scent of hay and mown grass and roses and dews and a thousand wild flowers, that I'm beginning to think of my South Sea wind [as] pale and scentless by comparison!"[5]

That was the summer that the Great War started. It was a season of European civilization that was long remembered, and that, in the remembering, was mythicized. The shattered world that lay dying in the trenches of the First World War looked back upon the golden, hazy summer of 1914 as an idyll that had proven to be unreal. The tranquillity of those last months of peacetime was seen as a deception, and their beauty came to be thought of as a lure used for betrayal. The summer of 1914 became the symbol of a certain kind of statement about the nature of European civilization that, in the bitterness of wartime, was thought to be a lie. "If any question why we died,/Tell them, because our fathers lied": so wrote Rudyard Kipling, expressing the common thought, in *Epitaphs of the War (1914-18)*. There were those who thought much the same thing when the Second World War took place, and others who thought it during the

---

[3]Henri Beraud, *Qu' As Tu Fait De Ta Jeunesse?* (Paris: Les Editions de France, 1941), p. 227.

[4]Paul Fussell, *The Great War and Modern Memory* (New York and London: Oxford University Press, 1975), pp. 23–24.

[5]Geoffrey Keynes, ed., *The Letters of Rupert Brooke* (New York: Harcourt Brace Jovanovich, 1968), p. 594.

devastating American involvement in Vietnam.

The light from overhead rockets seems to make it clear. In the fierce glare of modern international warfare,[6] the prewar assertion that mankind finally has become civilized always seems to stand exposed as a lie. As Henry James wrote to a friend on the first day after the British entered the Great War, "The plunge of civilization into this abyss of blood and darkness . . . is a thing that so gives away the whole long age during which we have supposed the world to be, with whatever abatement, gradually bettering, that to have to take it all now for what the treacherous years were all the while really making for and *meaning* is too tragic for any words."[7]

It was not merely that the outbreak of a world-wide war was unexpected, but that nobody was prepared for the new and terrible *type* of war that ensued. The gay and gallant mood in which the young went to the front was expressed in a letter that Rupert Brooke wrote to a friend at home: "Come and die. It'll be great fun."[8] An experience of the peculiar horrors of the war changed all that. The war poet Wilfred Owen spoke in the changed mood when he wrote that if one were to see what he had seen in the front lines, "My friend, you would not tell with such high zest / To children ardent for some desperate glory, / The old Lie: Dulce et decorum est / Pro patria mori."[9]

Glory and honor died in the trench warfare, amid mud, lice, rats, and stagnant pools. As Jean Renoir showed in his classic film *La Grande Illusion*, it was illusory to believe that chivalry could sur-

[6]By international warfare I mean that in which two or more belligerents claim to be independent. Thus the American Civil War was in my terms an international war.

[7]Quoted in Fussell, *The Great War*, p. 8.

[8]Quoted in Anatole Broyard, "The Poet as Hero," New York *Times*, January 24, 1981, p. 12.

[9]Wilfred Owen, "Dulce Et Decorum Est", in *The Collected Poems of Wilfred Owen*, edited by C. Day Lewis (New York: New Directions Books, 1964), p. 55.

3

vive the 1914 war. In some special branches of the armed services — military aviation in the First World War, and perhaps the desert tank corps in the Second World War — remnants of the old knightly traditions of warfare could be found. For the most part, they could not. Human beings used such weapons as poison gas against one another. Mass executions of civilians took place in Belgium and elsewhere. French troops bleated like sheep as they were sent to their slaughter.

No Man's Land became the visual symbol of the squalor and of the endless, pointless killing. Thousands would be killed with no greater result than the taking of a few extra feet of No Man's Land, which would then be lost again, with more killing. The longest battle in the history of the world was fought at Verdun in 1916, with the greatest density of dead per square yard that has ever been known, and yet there was little to show for it.[10] There, in an area a bit less than four square miles, 650,000 men were killed, wounded, or gassed in a period of ten months, with no significant gain of ground for either side, in an engagement that left both armies in substantially the same position as when they began.

Living underground for years, in the 25,000 miles of trenches they had dug on the western front, men gave up hope.[11] An historian recently has written that "the likelihood that peace would ever come again was often in serious doubt during the war. One did not have to be a lunatic or a particularly despondent visionary to conceive quite seriously that the war would literally never end and would become the permanent condition of mankind. The stalemate and the attrition would go on infinitely, becoming, like the telephone and the internal combustion engine, a part of the accepted atmosphere of the modern experience."[12]

When, in fact, the war did come to an end, it is no wonder that those who had survived the world of No Man's Land were

---

[10]Alistair Horne, *The Price of Glory: Verdun 1916* (New York: St. Martin's Press, 1963), p. 1.

[11]Fussell, *The Great War*, p. 37.

[12]Fussell, *The Great War*, p. 71.

determined never to return to it. In their poems, their letters, and their diaries, they wrote over and over again that they would expose the lie that it is a noble thing to kill or to die for one's country.

One of the reasons they thought that they could see to it that there would be no more wars was that everybody on all sides had suffered so much. It was reasonable to suppose that the citizens of all of the belligerent countries had learned from their suffering that anything was better than going to war again. It turned out, however, that such was not the case. In the 1920s, while leading Englishmen were writing pacifist tracts on behalf of the League of Nations, disgruntled Germans were reading Adolf Hitler's *Mein Kampf*. The victors thought that the war itself had been terrible; but the vanquished thought what was terrible about it was who had won it.

On the Allied side, it also was thought that everybody had used up their reserves of strength and heroism, and that it simply would not be possible to get troops to go through the wartime experience again. At Scott Fitzgerald's Dick Diver said, in *Tender is the Night,* "This Western-front business couldn't be done again, not for a long time. The young men think they could do it again but they couldn't." It seemed true enough at the time, but the 1940 war showed that, though true of the French, it was not true of the British or the Germans.

The program of the generation of 1914, which aimed at making the First World War the war to end all wars, rested on the premise that civilization before the war had been false and on the promise that honesty could put it right. It was not fully accurate on either count. The seeming civility of European life in 1914 certainly concealed a great deal from view, but Henry James was wrong to think that civilization in Britain and elsewhere had not been on the rise. The summer of 1914 did not represent so great a lie as all that. Its apparent calm masked the violent discontent of social forces within Great Britain itself, but it was not these internal British forces that plunged civilization in 1914 into the abyss of darkness of which Henry James wrote. The forces that did it were foreign. It was the occasional clash of alien Powers that intruded upon the peaceful lives of Henry James and his Anglo-American contemporaries. Life *within* the advanced countries of the world had indeed become more civilized—Henry James had been right to believe it in the first place, and was wrong to recant the belief later. It was *between* the independent states that the civilizing process had not advanced very much since the beginning of time. Henry James and others failed to see that in entering the domain of international politics they were straying outside the gates of the city into a No Man's Land where no writ runs and no ruler holds sway.

In that No Man's Land, the postwar League of Nations program of persuasion and conciliation proved to be of little effect. Leaders of opinion in Britain and the United States in the 1920s argued that what had been fundamentally wrong in world politics before the war was the general acceptance of warfare as an instrument of national policy. They claimed that if they could demonstrate to everyone that war was self-defeating, they could persuade the governments of the world to renounce its use. In any event, they made their demonstrations, their speeches, and their treaties abolishing warfare, to no avail.

Yet in one important respect, we continue to believe what they believed. The leaders of civilized opinion in every generation since 1914, and especially since the development of nuclear and other weapons of mass destruction, have believed that there is an urgent need for world politics to be transformed in such a fundamental way that warfare will be abolished and mankind will never have to go back into the trenches and the bomb shelters again. The question, of course, is how to do it. Each generation has thought it understood the flaws in the approach of its predecessor, and each has adopted an approach with flaws of its own. The United Nations was designed to overcome the failings of the League of Nations, and plans now abound for changes designed to overcome the failings of the United Nations.

In 1939, on the eve of the renewed war, the English historian E. H. Carr published a short book that, though it did not provide a satisfactory answer, asked the question more lucidly than it had ever been asked before. College students of international relations have read it, year after year, and continue to read it today. Carr wrote it at a time when Western leaders, such as Neville Chamberlain, in their quest for peace had made things worse rather than better. For his time, and for ours, Carr posed the question with which the following chapters will be concerned: Where had they all gone wrong?

2

THE QUESTION
BECOMES ACADEMIC

They went wrong at the very beginning. They made a false start. They adopted theoretical premises that were false. Those premises continue to be relied upon today. Thus the misunderstanding of international politics that has characterized the statements and actions of leaders of opinion and government in the Western world throughout the twentieth century goes back to the aftermath of the 1914–1918 war; and, because the field of international relations was developed in the university, it is a misunderstanding that is rooted in academic theory.

Leaders of the prevailing school of thought of the 1920s — which later was characterized and castigated as idealistic — included Gilbert Murray, Regius Professor of Greek at Oxford University; his son-in-law, the historian Arnold Toynbee; and a number of American professors of international law. The realist attack on idealism in the 1930s, 1940s, and 1950s also was led by professors, such as Carr in Britain, Morgenthau in America, and Aron in France. The attack on realism as unscientific, in the 1960s, was mounted by professors of the behavioral school of political science; and the counterattack against behavioralism has also been led by professors.

9

In the last couple of decades, it has become noticeable, at least in the United States, that academic figures are also being entrusted with key roles in the creation and execution of foreign policy. Among advisers on national security affairs to the president of the United States during these years, one thinks of W. W. Rostow and McGeorge Bundy, both of whom came to the government from university life, and Henry Kissinger and his successor, Zbigniew Brzezinski, both professors of international relations, as well as Richard Allen, who at one time was a member of the staff of the Hoover Institution at Stanford University. Foreign countries have followed the lead: among the foreign officials, for example, with whom Secretary Kissinger used to deal during his years in power were many who had attended the seminars he used to teach at Harvard in the field of international relations. These officials often carry into effect the theories, profit from the truths, and fall victim to the fallacies that they taught or learned in the classroom.

The issues also are defined for the American electorate by candidates guided in this respect by academic figures. Ever since the Adlai Stevenson presidential campaign in 1956 and the successful John F. Kennedy campaign of 1960, candidates for the presidency have relied upon groups of academics to provide them with advice, position papers, and material for speeches on foreign policy. The person appointed to report back to the candidate and summarize the advice that has been received is called by some such title as foreign policy coordinator, and usually is an academic figure. That was true in the campaigns of the last three candidates to successfully seek the presidency: Richard Allen served in the 1968 Nixon and the 1980 Reagan campaigns, while Zbigniew Brzezinski, who lost with Hubert Humphrey in 1968, won with Jimmy Carter in 1976.

The material supplied to the foreign policy coordinator comes largely from academic sources, if personal experience provides a reliable guide. I served as foreign policy coordinator for Hubert Humphrey in the 1972 presidential primary campaign, and the authorities whom the Humphrey staff asked me to consult were almost entirely in academic life, rather than persons whose careers had been in the State Department or in international law or international business. Senator Humphrey had such long experience that he could provide the practical perspective himself, but there have been other candidates for the presidency who lacked a foreign policy background, and who therefore have had to rely on the academic advisors for the words and concepts to frame the issues for the American public.

Once in office, the president is confronted by the need to coordinate the foreign policy of the administration with a body that also is guided by academic advice, the United States Senate. It is usual for a senator to have on the staff someone who recently has completed graduate or postgraduate studies in international relations, usually with the title of Legislative Assistant for Foreign Policy. To a lesser or greater degree, this staff member drafts speeches and articles on foreign policy in the senator's name, and advises the senator how to vote on foreign policy issues.

Foreign policy, then, is one area of practical activity in the United States in which academic theory matters significantly. What is taught in international relations courses, and how it is taught, actually affect lives and fortunes. This chapter, and two chapters that follow it, are devoted to matters of theory because they lead to the questions about the practical conduct of foreign policy that are discussed in Chapter 5.

At the outset, it should be noted that, at least in the United States, undergraduate courses in international affairs generally are taught by the textbook method, which is to say, that one or more textbooks are assigned to the students as their reading material. This is by no means the only, or even the obvious, way to teach a course that deals with the practical affairs of the world. Courses in business and in law are taught instead by the casebook method, in which actual cases are studied in order to learn in specific sets of circumstances what is done now and what ought to be done in the future. In international relations courses, students might be asked to learn about the conduct of world politics by studying in detail how the war crisis of 1878 was averted by the English foreign minister, the Marquis of Salisbury, in his Circular of April 1, 1878, or how the subsequent Congress of Berlin was successfully managed by the German leader, Otto von Bismarck. The current tendency, however, is to avoid the use even of historical examples; one of the most popular of the recent textbooks begins by saying that "no historical background is provided" and that the subject is to be taught instead by the "rigorous development of concepts and theories."[1] What this shows is the intention with which the study of international relations has been developed in the twentieth century. The international politics of the past are not to be emulated, for they are to be fundamentally changed. Students are not taught to be Salisburys and Bismarcks because Salisburys and Bismarcks are no longer wanted.

What They Teach

The concepts and theories that are applied to international relations are those of political science. In other words, the body of knowledge derived from studying relationships within states is applied to relationships between states, as though they were the same thing. This was made evident in the first of the major textbooks, Schuman's *International Politics*, which appeared in 1933. As its then subtitle proclaimed, it was *An Introduction to the Western State System*, and it began with a consideration of the state and its citizens. Schuman wrote that he proposed to deal with the subject from the point of view of political science, and that "This orientation assumes that the phenomena of international politics can be dealt with most fruitfully if they are envisaged as aspects of the whole pattern of political behavior and power

---

[1]William D. Coplin, *Introduction to International Politics: A Theoretical Overview* (Chicago: Markham Publishing Company, 1971), p. xv.

relations which has developed in Western civilization."[2] He carried through this program by identifying the cause of conflict within countries and the cause of wars between countries as complementary aspects of the same basic reality, which he thought to be class warfare; and, in Leninist fashion, he argued that international wars occur because the ruling classes in the various countries want new wealth and new markets.[3] In later editions, Schuman changed the subtitle of his text to *Anarchy and Order in the World Society,* and by the seventh (and last) edition he had considerably modified his views, but his basic political science orientation remained the same.

When E. H. Carr published his eloquent book in 1939 inquiring what had gone wrong in international affairs, he also did so against a background of theories and concepts derived from political science.

Hans Morgenthau, too, wrote from the point of view of political science. His textbook appeared in 1948 and rapidly overtook Schuman's in use and popularity. In its various editions (five, plus a fifth revised edition) it has been far and away the best seller in its field, according to sources in the publishing trade. A recent study has verified that it is still the textbook most frequently assigned to students in beginning international relations courses.[4] Morgenthau, too, pictured conflict within countries and conflict between countries as aspects of one underlying reality, which was politics itself, as he defined it: the struggle for power.

As new schools of thought arose in political science, they too were directly applied to international relations. The behavioral school, with its emphasis on systems theory and game theory, was only one of several to apply its teaching in this field. Thus a leading recent text is introduced by its author's claim that "I have

---

[2]Schuman, *International Politics,* pp. xii–xiii.
[3]Schuman, *International Politics,* p. 847.
[4]James N. Rosenau et al., "Of Syllabi, Texts, Students, and Scholarships in International Relations: Some Data and Interpretations on the State of a Burgeoning Field," *World Politics,* January 1977, pp. 263–340.

tried to relate the field of international politics to the mainstream of concepts currently in use by political scientists."[5]

What They Ignore

Yet from the time of its origin in the teachings of Plato, political science has avoided dealing with what is fundamental in international relations. Initially, this was because Socrates and Plato discussed politics in terms of an imaginary ideal state. A distinguished classicist has written that "the sole form of political thought originally recognized by Aristotle was that handed down by Plato, the Utopia"; and, "It is significant that one of his criticisms of Plato's ideal states is that they take no account of foreign affairs."[6] It has remained a characteristic of utopian literature ever since that the ideal state is so situated, on a remote island or in an inaccessible valley, that the rest of the world can be safely ignored. The most famous of modern utopians, Karl Marx, achieved the same theoretical result in a different way: in his vision, the state would dissolve, which in turn would cause interstate relations to disappear.[7] Utopia never has a foreign policy.

Even after political science outgrew utopianism, political science continued to ignore the fundamental reality of international relations, which is that the corporate entities that are its principal actors are independent of higher authority. *This is not a phenomenon that occurs within countries, and so political science does not deal with it.* E. H. Carr failed to see that it was the ignoring of this central reality that had led the theorists of international

---

[5]Coplin, *International Politics*, pp. xvii–xviii.

[6]Werner Jaeger, *Aristotle: Fundamentals of the History of His Development*, translated by Richard Robinson, 2nd Ed. (London: Oxford University Press, 1948), pp. 263, 288.

[7]Originally it was Marx's view that the state would be dissolved as a result of universal suffrage. David McLellan, *Karl Marx: His Life and Thought* (London: Macmillan, 1973), p. 75. Later Marx came to believe that the state would wither away as a result of the achievement of a classless society.

relations astray. An understanding of the meaning of independence is fundamental to an understanding of international relations. It is that fundamental matter to which we should turn now.

The Meaning of Independence

Independence is the aspect of freedom that is negative. It means that an entity is not ruled by anybody else, that there is no entity above it, no political superior, no authority it recognizes and obeys. It is a special case: it describes a state of political affairs that is found only in international relations.

In this context, whether or not an entity is independent is a question of fact. The relevant question is whose orders, in case of conflict, are obeyed. If the government of Algeria gives its people an order, and if any other government or political authority gives a contrary order, the people of Algeria will follow the order given by their own leaders; and that is what is meant by saying that Algeria is independent. It does not mean that Algeria is free to do whatever it chooses. Like any other country, it is the prisoner of its circumstances: for example, its geography, its relative power, its relative wealth, the nature and number of its inhabitants, and the disposition of its neighbors. Independence means only the freedom to choose between such alternatives as fate may offer, few and disagreeable though these may be.

This has been a frustrating discovery for many of the poorer countries of Asia, Africa, and the Caribbean, newly liberated from colonial rule, and having won their freedom with high hopes for what it would bring. They have found, for example, that to obtain financial credits from international agencies such as the International Monetary Fund, they must submit to conditions they regard as onerous and that in effect constitute dictation to them of how they must run their own economies. Independence entitles them to reject such terms. But, in context, they may regard this freedom as a mockery, as something purely formal and without real content; they may see it as merely the freedom to starve.

In a sense that is true: independence is the right to choose, but it does not bring with it a guarantee that any of the available choices will be acceptable. Two thousand years ago, the kingdom of Judaea was unable to withstand the military power of the Romans, and the last of its defenders, at the fortress of Masada, chose to commit suicide rather than submit. Theirs was the most narrowly limited of freedoms; but within those limits they were free. Their decision to kill themselves was the ultimate result of their refusal to accept the orders of the Roman government instead of their own and as such was the definition of what made Judaea independent.

Every state is independent. But no human being is — or ever has been. Except for hermits who live and die alone in the desert, the life of every person is lived in the context of a group. This difference between the way individuals live and the way that states live has been a continuing source of misunderstanding in the study of political affairs

Important political theories, in the seventeenth and eighteenth centuries, and more recently too, have started from the premise that human beings once lived as ungoverned individuals, in a state of primitive anarchy. Some have imagined this as a state of nature in which every person was at war with every other person. In turn, this savage state of nature was analogized to the international situation of the modern world; and from the analogy conclusions were drawn about the nature and destiny of world politics.

The truth, according to scientists today, is quite different and more complicated.[8] Evidences of the life of man-like creatures going back millions of years show that, even then, human existence

---

[8]David Fromkin, *The Question of Government: An Inquiry Into the Breakdown of Modern Political Systems* (New York: Charles Scribner's Sons, 1975).

fell into a pattern of group activity. The circumstances of human evolution over the course of perhaps a million generations show that human beings had to function in groups from the very beginning in order to survive. Ethologists have observed the germs of group life and organization even in chimpanzees and other primates closely related to humans. Thus the hypothesis of primitive beginnings in which each individual was on his own has been invalidated. Always and everywhere, human beings function in groups — groups, moreover, that have at least some elements of organization, in terms of rules and leadership, however informal or minimal these may be. There is, after all, honor even among thieves.

When Aristotle tells us that "man is by nature an animal intended to live in a *polis*," and when, in 1978, an excavator of the most ancient prehistoric sites tells us that it is of the essence of human nature to engage in food sharing, both are stressing aspects, albeit different ones, of the proposition that it is the nature of a human being to belong to a group.[9] It is the nature of a state, on the contrary, not to belong to a group, but rather to be independent.

Thus it is important to differentiate relations between people, who as members of a group are bound by a common ethic, and relations between the alien corporate entities that are states. That is something that E. H. Carr in his famous book *The Twenty Years' Crisis* denied. He admitted that the personality of the state was a fiction; but he asserted that it was necessary to postulate it anyway.[10] He argued that it was necessary because only in this way could one clearly express the moral and legal responsibility of states for their actions. It was an argument that betrayed its own error, for states, being independent, do not have legal obligations in the same sense that fellow citizens do, and it was the confusion of the different senses in which the word "law" can be used that

---

[9] Aristotle *Politics* 7.2 1253a9; Glynn Isaac, "The Food-Sharing Behavior of Protohuman Hominids," *Scientific American*, Vol. 238 (April 1978), p. 90.
    [10] Carr, *Crisis*, pp. 189 et seq.

had characterized the unrealistic idealism of the 1920s and 1930s which Carr, in his book, undertook to attack. The unrealistic idealists had thought that if Nazi Germany did not live up to its obligation to the world community to behave peacefully, it would find itself in much the same situation that a person would be who broke the laws of a particular country by committing rape or murder. Carr wrote his book in part to explain why these two situations are different. It was a major flaw in his otherwise brilliant performance that he undermined his case by arguing that states should be thought about as though they were persons.

When Carr came to explain the difference between the law that applies to states and the law that applies to persons who live within the same country, he wrote that the former lacks three institutions: "a judicature, an executive, and a legislature."[11] Carr apparently did not see that this adds up to more than just a "lack." These three — the executive, the legislative, and the judiciary — are the three parts of government. It is no accident that states are not subject to them. The aspects of world government do not exist because a world government does not exist.

The most important political fact about individual human beings is that they live in groups and are subject to the government and the laws of their group. Pretending that states are like people enabled Carr and others to imply that states, too, owe allegiance to a higher political authority and owe obedience to a body of laws. This pretense resulted from a fear that is at any rate understandable. The independence of states is so frightening that the natural reaction is to turn away from it. That, I suppose, is why the concept of independence, in the United States for example, is relegated to Fourth of July parades and why it is pretended that independence means freedom from only those restraints that are deplorable (such as the tyranny imposed by colonial empires). But it means more than that: it means freedom from any normative restraint whatsoever.

---

[11]Carr, *Crisis*, p. 219.

Dostoyevsky's Ivan Karamazov's assertion was that if human beings were not restrained by a belief in immortality, nothing would be immoral and anything would be permitted, even cannibalism; and that in these circumstances, people ought to act out of self-interest even if it leads them to crime.[12] As a practical matter, that is not true with respect to individual humans; whatever their beliefs may be about immortality, they are restrained by civic loyalties and by the civil authorities. But it is a reasonably true statement about states. At their worst, states are beasts that roam the jungles of world politics, killing when they are hungry, and obeying no laws but those of their own nature. Where they are concerned, Dostoyevsky's terrible words ring true: anything is permitted.

But whereas Ivan Karamazov feared what he himself might do if unrestrained, in international relations it is the freedom of others that is most frightening. There is no protection against the others except self-defense. No matter how extreme and unwarranted may be the cruelties that states inflict, there is no context to give either meaning or effect to the notion of punishment. There is justice within our respective states, but there is no justice between the states. In the dark streets and alleyways that the states of the world roam, the least convincing of all cries is the victim's impotent threat that "you can't get away with this!" — for countries, if they are strong enough, can get away with anything.

Of course, there are limits to the freedom of action of independent states, but from the point of view of justice and morality, these limits are irrelevant. They are such morally accidental limitations as relative strength, resources, and geographical location. They do not correspond to the limitations that domestic societies impose upon their members, because they are not imposed by a superior authority, let alone a superior authority who is morally purposeful. They are merely a form of

[12]Fyodor Dostoyevsky, *The Brothers Karamazov*, Part 1, Book 2, Chapter 6.

trial by combat, and the results of trial by combat are not necessarily just. Indeed it is one of the attributes of justice — genuine justice — that it does exactly the reverse; that it protects the weak against the strong, and that on appeal, it reverses the results of those of life's trials that are by combat, rather than by reason, in the search for truth, mercy, and fairness.

International affairs are constantly a surprise because our expectations about politics are conditioned by the experience of living within a political entity. Within that entity we expect and to a certain extent obtain physical security and justice, and the benefits of programs to ensure our welfare. There is a tendency to approach international affairs with similar expectations, but the expectations prove to be false. Among states, there is no justice for the weak, no security even for the strong, and often no aid for the needy. World politics do not provide the satisfactions that can be obtained in national politics and that have come to be thought of as mankind's due. It is not because of the wickedness or stupidity of leadership groups that the satisfactions are not obtained; it is because world affairs do not have a unitary political structure.

The world of independent nations is, therefore, most unsatisfactory: its methods, its goals, and its characteristic solutions to problems are not what we would wish them to be. The characteristics of international politics — the lack of a political structure, the lack of justice, the inevitability of wars — are repugnant to civilized values and human ideals. Yet we must recognize them for what they are if we are to function effectively in their domain. It is only against the background of such a recognition that we can turn to the questions that so much troubled E. H. Carr, such as the relation between morality and power in international affairs, and find that answering them is relatively easy.

Power Politics

When the government of Nazi Germany successfully bullied the

20

world in the 1930s, observers of international affairs concluded that power played a greater role in the world's affairs, and morality a lesser one, than they had previously believed. Carr spoke not merely for himself, but for a whole disillusioned generation, when he wrote, "Politics are, then, in one sense always power politics."[13]

After the Second World War, when the German threat had been replaced by the Soviet one, Hans Morgenthau systematically applied this perception in his textbook to the description of world politics. He portrayed international relations in all times and places as the expression of power politics. His picture of international politics was masterly and realistic, but his explanation of *why* it was so was unconvincing. He wrote that international politics are power politics because *all* politics are power politics. Anyone can see this is untrue in terms of the politics we know best, the politics of our own country. We can see that not all domestic American politics are power politics, that there are other kinds of politics, too. And we can see that in our domestic politics, the justification for playing power politics does not exist.

Within an organized and civilized political community, such as ours, a person ought not to need to have any power. He ought not to need it in order to physically survive, for his government purports to enclose him within a matrix of security. Police and other armed forces are supposed to protect him from harm. The judiciary and the other branches of government are supposed to insure that his interests receive due consideration and are not treated unfairly. Welfare, health, and educational programs provide positive benefits that go far beyond mere protection. One should be able to live, thrive, and be happy without being powerful.

In a democracy, such as our own, it also is not necessary to be powerful in order to have an equal vote in determining who will govern the country. We are enfranchised as of right. It is a right

_____

[13]Carr, *Crisis*, p. 131.

that should give us all the power that we legitimately need, for, as Abraham Lincoln is quoted as having said, "The ballot is stronger than the bullet." Since it is not necessary to seek power, we are suspicious, and rightly so, of anyone who does seek it. Undue concentration of powers is perceived as a danger to the commonwealth, and we have enacted legislation that is designed to inhibit it, forbid it, or regulate it. Persons are not supposed to seek public office merely for purposes of self aggrandizement; we like to believe that those who seek office do so in order to accomplish what they believe to be in the public interest.

Within this context, it is proper to draw a distinction between politics as the pursuit of power and politics in support of a program. The distinction is valid because it is not always necessary to take power in order to enact one's program; sometimes it is even the reverse that is the case. In recent American politics, it is the prevailing view that only a right-wing Republican like Richard Nixon could have succeeded in carrying out the liberal Democratic program of entering into relations with communist China. Similarly, two decades ago in France, it was only General de Gaulle, as the champion of national grandeur, who was able to win his country's backing for conceding independence to Algeria. Clearly there are times when you can best accomplish what you desire by having your opponents take power; the ideal may be, in Disraeli's phrase, "Tory men and Whig measures."

Moreover, in domestic politics a great deal of what goes on is the pursuit of *influence* rather than the pursuit of power. Washington lobbyists, presidential advisers, television personalities, and newspaper editorialists play an important role even though they hold no official position in the shaping of American national decisions. To influence a decision requires a different ability from that to make a decision, but in internal affairs both are parts of the political process.

It is not so in international affairs. In politics among nations, there is no influence without power. There is also no enfranchisement as of right; there is no entitlement to a voice or a vote in the making of international decisions. A state cannot advance its views except through the use of its power. A state cannot exist unless it has the power to compel other states to recognize its sovereign independence. There is no world government to guarantee and secure the rights of states or the inviolability of their frontiers or even their bare survival.

Thus the first and essential condition that enables an entity to exist and participate in international politics — which is to say, to be an independent state — is the possession of an adequate amount of power. That is the price of independence. What this means is that, in the first instance, all *international* politics necessarily are power politics, for only if a state achieves at least a minimum amount of success in power politics can it go on to engage in any other kind of politics. This condition of existence is what all states have in common with one another. Their response to this condition was described by Hans Morgenthau when he wrote that what states have to do, before they can do anything else, is to attempt to pursue their national interests as defined in terms of power.

The national interest means different things to different governments. Yet Morgenthau's generalized description remains meaningful. It is true that governments define the national interest of their respective states with varying degrees of wisdom and accuracy, and that the measures they take in pursuit of the national interest also vary. At the simplest level, however, there are imperatives that all governments recognize. For example, a leading British scholar has written, "It is doubtful whether there is any instance in history of a power disarming unilaterally and voluntarily;" even if one could find such an example, it would be a mere curiosity, for it is clear that countries, since the beginning of history, have recognized that they need to have armed forces in order to survive.[14]

---

[14]Martin Wight, *Power Politics,* edited by Hedley Bull and Carsten Holbraad (New York: Holmes & Meier, Royal Institute of International Affairs, 1968), p. 260.

Armed force, of course, is only one kind of power. Power can mean many things. Japan is a great industrial Power, Saudi Arabia is a great petroleum Power, and the Soviet Union is a great military Power. All of them are powerful, but in such different ways that perhaps one should not use the same word to describe all three. Power can mean the resources that a nation has at its command: its military forces, the skill of its leadership, its wealth, and such things as these. But it can also refer to the state of affairs that its resources make possible, such as its independence or its influence over domestic or foreign events. Power can be thought of as a means, as an end, or as both. Some make the distinction, too, between the power that a state expresses by successfully asserting and maintaining its own independence, and the kind of power that it seeks when it tries to exercise dominion over others. Hans Morgenthau frequently has been criticized for not distinguishing between the different senses in which he employs the concept of power, but in large part the confusion of meanings inheres in the English language and is difficult to avoid.

What the concept of the national interest as defined in terms of power enabled Morgenthau to do was to point to the common denominator of international relations. It enabled him to write the first textbook in this field that was scientific, in the sense that it measured all states by the same yardstick. A letter written in about 1750 B.C. to the king of Mari, near what is now the frontier between Syria and Iraq, reads: "There is no king who is powerful on his own. Ten to fifteen kings follow Hammurabi, king of Babylon; a like number Rim-Sin, king of Larsa; a like number Ibal-pi-el, king of Eshnunna; a like number Amut-pi-el, king of Qatna, while twenty kings follow Yarim-Lim, king of Yamkhat."[15] Thus four millennia ago, the king of Mari engaged in the same line of business as did Talleyrand and Bismarck later, and as do Henry Kissinger and Alexander Haig today; the con-

---

[15]Theophile James Meek, *Hebrew Origins* (New York, Evanston, and London: Harper & Row, Harper Torchbooks/The Cloister Library, 1960), p. 3.

24

cerns of the king of Mari were similar to our own. It was Morgenthau's illuminating theory that these concerns are what states have
in common.

What remained to be done was to explain why this is so — why
states pursue power interests and why international politics can
most accurately be defined as power politics. As long as international relations were thought of in political-science terms, rather
than in their own terms, no satisfactory explanation was possible.
Independence makes all the difference. It is *because* states are independent that inter-state relations are power politics; in this and
other respects, international politics are not, contrary to what
Hans Morgenthau taught, like other kinds of politics: they are
unique.

Moral Politics

Thus all international politics are power politics because states are
independent, and in support of their independence must pursue
interests that are literally vital. Yet, to the extent that the realities
of power permit them to do so, governments sometimes go on,
quite rightly, to act in accordance with the moral views of their
constituents. It is also politically wise of them to do so, not merely
in terms of helping the government to remain in office, but also
in terms of strengthening a country's foreign policy by mobilizing
popular support behind it.

Morality, then, plays a role in international politics; but in
domestic politics it plays not one but two roles. One role, which
morality plays in both domestic and international politics, is that
it sometimes motivates the actors: persons and governments at
times do things because they think they are the right things to do.
A second role, played only in domestic politics, not in international politics, is that the community is animated as a whole to
impose its moral code even upon those who disagree. In a country such as our own, in which the government plays an active
role, it, as a higher authority, carries into effect a system of values

25

based on the community's moral code. It does so by making, interpreting, and enforcing various rules. When, for example, Americans came to view child labor as vicious, our government forbade it. That is the process by which a widespread subjective opinion about moral values gains an objective public expression.

In international affairs, this cannot happen. To begin with, there is no moral code that is agreed upon in common by all the peoples and governments of the world; what seems right to Russians may seem wrong to Americans. Then there is no real higher authority, no substantive world government, to articulate, interpret, and impose moral values, so that in international affairs the process objectively realizing such values cannot take place.

Is there no way, then, to oppose the wrongful conduct and the oppressive power of others in international relations? For the generation of the 1930s, threatened by Nazi Germany, that was a real and immediate question. For us, threatened by the growth of Soviet power, it is a question that is real today, and, many believe, one that is immediate, too.

There is no way for the world to deal with the wrongful conduct of states as such, for there is no world community to define what constitutes wrongfulness and no world political community to impose such a definition upon the states that disagree with it. But there may be ways to deal with *power;* the academics who developed the study of international relations attempted to come to grips with them. Indeed a principal endeavor of those who, in the 1930s and 1940s, rediscovered the important role that power plays in world politics was to find what restraints might prove effective against it. The structure of an international relations book at the time was typically like this: the first section would describe the role of force and power in international affairs; the middle section would discuss international law, morality, and public opinion as restraints of power; and the final section would offer a plan for transforming international relations in such a way that power would matter less, justice would matter more, and peace would be preserved more of the time.

The question of whether the primacy of power in international relations is tempered by the force of ethics or justice is not a new inquiry. It is at least as old as the section in Thucydides' history of the Peloponnesian War that has come to be known as the Melian dialogue, written 2,500 years ago. In the moral vision of Thucydides, the strong who are reckless eventually bring ruin upon themselves, but in the meantime there is nothing to protect the weak against them. E. H. Carr, unlike Thucydides, was unwilling to stare unblinkingly into the face of reality. Like the Melians, whose misplaced faith in the power of goodness led to their doom, Carr refused to believe that the gods would be so unjust as to abandon the weak to the wicked. He wrote that "The fact that national propaganda everywhere so eagerly cloaks itself in ideologies of a professedly international character proves the existence of an international stock of common ideas, however limited and however weakly held, to which appeal can be made, and of a belief that these common ideas stand somehow in the scale of values above national interests."[16]

But talk is cheap, and the lip service that propaganda pays to virtue has no practical consequence if a state does not in fact practice the morality that it preaches. Morality is a force only if it leads to action and not to mere words. If Carr could have shown that states modify their conduct to bring their behavior into line with their propaganda, he would have been able to make his case; but he did not have any convincing examples of this to cite. His authority for the proposition that modern states would hesitate to engage in actions that were unjust was, oddly enough, *Mein Kampf.* Carr wrote that, "As Herr Hitler says, 'every persecution which lacks a spiritual basis' has to reckon with the opposition that this will arouse."[17] But there is no evidence that Hitler let this deter him from embarking on his own persecutions.

Carr went on to quote Joseph Goebbels and Benito Mussolini

---

[16]Carr, *Crisis,* p. 185.
[17]Carr, *Crisis,* p. 184

to the effect that what Nazi Germany and Fascist Italy sought was international comity and a world in which all could enjoy the benefits of justice, security, and peace. Carr wrote that "nobody who knows the countries in question will doubt that both leaders and people are sincerely and passionately concerned to justify their policy in the light of universal standards of international morality."[18]

Carr was wrong in his assessment of the goals of Nazi Germany and Fascist Italy, and it was not an isolated, or merely a specific, mistake. It was his general proposition that was wrong: the proposition that moral protestations and verbal justifications have an improving effect upon the conduct of those who voice them. Carr was wrong in thinking that when Hitler appealed to moral standards, he consequently would restrain his use of Germany's power in line with these standards. The political function of moral appeals such as Hitler's is to deceive others. Even the most savage leaders find it desirable to make false statements about their actions and their intentions in order to make them more acceptable to others. Carr had misunderstook the function of propaganda in international politics; it is not its function to tell the truth.

The matter was put much more accurately by Hans Morgenthau:

> To what extent the profession of universalistic principles of morality can go hand in hand with utter depravity in action is clearly demonstrated in the case of Timur, the Mongol would-be conqueror of the world, who in the fourteenth century conquered and destroyed southern Asia and Asia Minor. After having killed hundreds of thousands of people — on December 12, 1398, he massacred one hundred thousand Hindu prisoners before Delhi — for the glory of God and of Mohammedanism, he said to a representative of conquered Aleppo: "I am not a man of blood; and God is my witness that in all my wars I have never been the aggressor, and that my enemies have always been the authors of their own calamity."

---

[18]Carr, *Crisis,* p. 198.

28

Gibbon, who reports this statement, adds: "During this peaceful conversation the streets of Aleppo streamed with blood, and re-echoed with the cries of mothers and children, with the shrieks of violated virgins. The rich plunder that was abandoned to his soldiers might stimulate their avarice; but their cruelty was enforced by the peremptory command of producing an adequate number of heads, which, according to his custom, were curiously piled in columns and pyramids. . . ."[19]

But it is not just the Timurs and Hitlers of this world who fail to put into practice the morality that they profess. In Carr's view, his own leaders, and those of the other enlightened Western European states, did the same thing. In the first edition of his book, in passages that were later deleted, Carr argued that the Versailles treaty had been unjust to Germany and that, by the 1930s, the leaders of England and France had recognized that this was the case. He contended that when the Western European powers acquiesced so easily in the expansionist steps taken by Hitler's Germany, such as the reoccupation of the Rhineland and the annexation of Austria, it was in part because of a consensus that these changes were in themselves reasonable and just. In Great Britain, he said, the reoccupation of the Rhineland was not merely tolerated by public opinion, but positively welcomed. Similarly, the Pact that Hitler negotiated with Chamberlain and the other European leaders at Munich in 1938 changed the Versailles arrangements to make them correspond, according to Carr, to accepted canons of international morality. Yet each of these changes had been won by Hitler through the use or threat of force. Carr reproached his own leaders with having failed to treat Germany according to their own notions of justice and morality in the years when Germany was powerless, and with having conceded what they themselves thought was Germany's due only when Hitler forced them to do so. He wrote that, from Germany's point

---

[19]Hans J. Morgenthau, *Politics Among Nations: The Struggle for Power and Peace,* 5th Ed., Rev. (New York: Alfred A. Knopf, 1978), p. 262.

of view, "There was not, even as late as 1936, any reasonable prospect of obtaining major modifications of the Versailles Treaty by peaceful negotiation unsupported by the ultimatum or the *fait accompli.*" Thus Hitler's Germany was "not without reason" in having become "almost wholly disillusioned about the role of morality in international affairs."[20]

That Carr may have been wrong about the injustice of Versailles and about the nature of Hitler's policy is beside the point. What is here relevant is that Carr claimed that on the basis of historical experience, Germany was justified in concluding that morality did not play a significant role in international affairs. If so, then Carr had shown that he himself was wrong in claiming that morality *does* play a significant role in limiting the dominion of power in international affairs.

He failed to see, therefore, that in the absence of self-restraint, power, in international affairs, is limited only by countervailing power. Thus the focus of concern in the study of international relations properly should fall on power and on the interplay of powers, not because power is the only factor (which it is not) but because without it the other factors would not come into play. The creation and maintenance of power, the elements of power, the comparative evaluation of power, the patterns and dynamics of the distribution of power: these are the matters that are the primary substance of the study of international relations because they form the first priority in the practice of international relations.

The nine or more senses in which the term "balance of power" is used thus assume fundamental relevance.[21] Certain recurring patterns in international relations become especially meaningful. A typical such pattern is this: the strongest state in a constellation of states seeks to dominate the others, is opposed by an alliance

---

[20]Carr, *Crisis*, p. 281.

[21]Martin Wight, "The Balance of Power," in *Diplomatic Investigations*, edited by Herbert Butterfield and Martin Wight (Cambridge: Harvard University Press, 1968), pp. 149, 151.

which this causes the other states to create, and (a) is defeated by the alliance, and forced to accept the peace terms which issue from a conference or congress of the victors, or (b) defeats the alliance, and annexes the defeated states to form an empire. The possibility that the outcome of extremist policies might be (a) can be used, as it was by European statesmen in the nineteenth century, to temper national ambitions.

The pattern that, as a result, emerged in the nineteenth century was not entirely unsatisfactory from the point of view of limiting the power of states. It was an equilibrium that expressed a culture and an outlook shared in common. Its political manifestation was self-restraint; and its political technique was restraint by the power of others, and the knowledge that aggrandizement was self-defeating, because it roused up combinations of other powers to oppose it. Hans Morgenthau quoted with approval this description of Europe before 1914: "The States were so bounded and organized that aggression could not succeed unless it was moderated and so directed that the prevailing opinion of the Powers approved it."[22] Thus a cultural consensus, working through the balancing of powers against powers, resulted in political stability on the basis of political consensus.

Morgenthau rightly concluded that certain civilized values, such as moderation and relative stability, therefore, could be achieved in international politics; but it could be done not by pretending that the role of power is a restricted one, but by making use of the restraints that only power can impose on power.

This is not to say that morality plays no role in international affairs. The purposes in the service of which the various states employ their power often express their respective moral concerns. Moreover, there is a sort of morality in the nature of the power struggle itself. It is the internal morality that inheres in the workings of power relationships. It can be understood most clearly in terms of those concepts of classical Greece in general, and of

---

[22]Morgenthau, *Politics,* pp. 226–227.

Thucydides in particular, that held that *hubris* leads to destruction, and that a goddess called Nemesis punishes human presumption. If a state accumulates or uses power immoderately, it thereby leads other states to combine against it with the intention of defeating or destroying it; and against the background of Greek concepts, it can be seen that this is an observation that is not merely of political, but also of moral, significance.

For teachers and students of international relations, however, this has not been enough, and the failure of morality to play the role that it does within the politics of our own countries has been a continuing source of disappointment to them. They regard the state of world politics as, in this respect, unhealthy, and the question they have pursued is: how can it be cured?

3

AT THE WRONG SPA

In the earlier part of this century, large numbers of Europeans strongly used to believe, as some still do, in the curative and restorative powers of certain mineral waters, such as those to be found at Spa in Belgium. But it was believed important to match the mineral water with the malady: the waters of some spas cured the liver, others rheumatism, still others, asthmatic disorders. The range of illnesses with which the watering-spots purported to deal was wide, and each spa had its special properties. It was necessary to choose the spa that was right for the specific ailment, because if one suffered from a particular disorder, waters that cured only another sort of disorder would prove useless.

That is what befell the academic and other figures who developed the study of international relations in the twentieth century and who sought to cure what they considered to be the disorders of world politics. They sought help from the same sources that they had used before, somewhat successfully, in dealing with the problem of how to resolve the competing and conflicting claims of individuals and groups within a state. From such sources they derived a wisdom that has proven to be inapplicable to international relations because of the independence of states, and also because of their corporate character. What they had learned earlier was useful, but not for the matter at hand. They were taking the waters at the wrong spa.

During the 1920s and the 1930s, when international relations began to emerge as an academic subject in its own right, the intellectual climate was favorable to interdisciplinary studies and references. It was very much the done thing to consult experts in other academic fields in hopes that they could shed new light upon one's own. Scholars reminded themselves and others that politics are grounded in human nature; and it followed that the whole range of social and natural sciences could be brought to bear upon the study of political science. It was only to be expected that these sciences would also be applied to the emerging academic field of international relations; and indeed it is characteristic of theories about international relations, especially at the time, that they refer to what Freud wrote about the ambiguities of the human soul and what Heisenberg taught about the indeterminancies of the universe, as though such concepts were directly relevant to an understanding of world politics.

Frederick L. Schuman's textbook *International Politics* provides an outstanding example of this sort of approach. In its first edition, Schuman's text began only as far back as the origins of civilization. In subsequent editions it begins with a discussion of the origin of the universe, then the makeup of the human personality and the origin of the species, and goes on to provide a panoramic view of the history of the human race. It is brilliantly done. The editors of *Foreign Affairs* recently wrote of it, in retrospect, that "it seems to combine the learning of Gibbon, the pragmatism of Machiavelli, the pessimism of Spengler and the indignation of Swift."[1] Yet it goes wrong because its references are to the sciences that deal with individual human beings rather

---

[1] Byron Dexter, ed., *The Foreign Affairs 50-Year Bibliography: New Evaluations of Significant Books on International Relations, 1920-1970* (New York and London: R. R. Bowker Company, 1972), p. 15.

than to the sciences that deal with the behavior of *groups* of human beings; and it is not the former but the latter with which the study of international relations is directly concerned. Psychology is a case in point. Schuman's discussion of personality problems was out of place in a discussion of the behavior of states, as was his borrowing of such terms as the Id and the Libido, because states do not have personalities, disordered or otherwise, nor do they have Ids or Libidos. Yet the range of his references and of his learning was so dazzling that readers were blinded to its irrelevance. Schuman established the pattern, to which theorists of international relations have adhered ever since, of consulting experts in the wrong fields, that is, those not directly relevant, or, in some cases, not relevant at all, to the relations between states.

The focus of inquiry in the field of international relations, for Schuman, as for Carr and for Morgenthau, and for those who followed them, was, and is, how the characteristics of international relations can be changed. It is a peculiarity of this academic field that those who study it dislike the facts that are its subject matter. I do not think that this is true of the students of any other field. Anatomists do not hate the structure of the body. Archaeologists do not loathe the civilizations that they uncover. Astronomers do not regard the shape of the galaxies as unsatisfactory; nor do they propose to rearrange the stars into a less displeasing pattern. But almost all students of the structure (or rather, the lack of structure) of international relations disapprove of that lack. They regard it as probably bad and certainly dangerous. They want to change the nature of international relations.

War is the manifestation of international relations of which they most disapprove, and therefore the question of why wars are fought—a major question with which the theory of international relations is concerned—is asked in order to learn how wars can be prevented. The answer has been sought in the findings of psychologists, sociologists, ethologists, biologists, and prehistorians with respect to the interrelationship of human individuals. These findings have been used, by Schuman and others, in an effort to understand what it is in human nature that causes the outbreak of wars. Thus Schuman claimed that the reintegration of the human personality would stop the destructive trend in world politics—which is to say, the tendency to fight wars.

Pessimists, citing Freud and others, claim that wars result from aggressive instincts that have deep biological and psychological roots. The writings of ethologists such as Konrad Lorenz are used to support this view, in the belief that animal behavior sheds light on human behavior. Optimists persuasively claim that, on the contrary, studies of earliest man by Richard Leakey and others show that the tendencies to share and cooperate are basic to the human species.

As Kenneth Waltz showed in *Man, The State and War*, what is wrong with discussing the matter in these terms is that the nature of individual human beings is not of any direct relevance to the question of why wars are fought, because individual human beings do not wage wars against one another. Englishmen do not generally make war against other Englishmen, and they did not have to wait until the human personality was reintegrated before this state of internal peace and order was reached. Individuals normally live, within their respective countries, without warring against one another.[2] The psychology of individuals, and the sociology of individuals within society, may be able to show us why there is domestic peace, but they are inapplicable to the question of why there is international war.

To understand international wars or any other kinds of international relations, one has to look at the units that are involved in international politics—and these are not individual humans but politically independent groups. Only in earlier times, when decisions commonly were made for a country by its king or some other solitary ruler, would the science of individual psychology have

---

[2]In the industrial countries of the modern world, revolutions and civil wars are relatively rare.

been relevant to a general study of international relations. One would have wanted to know about the drives and motivations and emotional and mental processes of the rulers who were making the decisions. The alleged drunkenness of Alexander, if true, and the undoubted lechery of Henry of Navarre were then the psychological stuff of which international politics were made. In city-state democracies, such as those of Greece in the fifth century B.C., where decisions were made by an assembly of the whole citizenry, the psychology of crowds, as discussed in such modern works as those of Gustave Le Bon, would have been a relevant study. In the modern world, however, the question of who makes decisions and how they are made is more complex, and requires many other sorts of knowledge. The mistake, which everybody makes at one time or another, of personifying nations, shoves these issues under the rug. When we ask what France *wants* or what England *thinks,* we have posed false questions that prevent the real questions from emerging. The personification of nations leads to an unthinking personification of their motives and decision-making processes. When states are spoken of as though they were people, they are said to lust, to grow angry, or to be consumed with envy — things that *states* cannot do. It is a mistake that is obvious, but it is nonetheless widespread; and it ought to be guarded against.

Decision-making for a state is a process much different from that for an individual. For one thing, an individual making a decision is identical with the individual on whose behalf the decision is made. With states it is otherwise, for the group constituting the government makes decisions on behalf of the whole population; and perhaps the most important thing to observe about a modern state is that those who make the governmental decisions are not identical with, nor are they necessarily representative of, the population as a whole. Those who govern may represent a special faction, class, or point of view. Their interests may not be the same as those of the rest of the population. A man or woman who makes a personal decision is at one with the self for whom the decision is made, and is unlikely to suffer from conflicts of interest; but those who govern make decisions for others whose welfare may matter little to the governors, or whose welfare might be conceived of in terms that are open to disagreement. Another difference is that a person's decisions are the result of one person's thought processes, whereas a group's decisions result from the interaction of the thoughts, words, and actions of many. The motives and intentions that go into the making of a group decision are various; and often it is difficult to predict what decisions will be made.

A special and especially important observation about group decisions in the domain of international relations is that such decisions frequently are made for reasons of domestic politics. The decisions are made, in other words, for reasons irrelevant to the matter at issue, but highly relevant to an extraneous matter. Thus the nature of states, which is so easily and falsely assumed to be like that of persons, is problematical and makes analysis and prediction difficult.

In the United States, an inquiry into the process by which national decisions about foreign policy are made would include questions about the role and interrelationships of the president, his staff, the president's personal advisers, his cabinet, the executive departments and the rival factions within them, the Congress, the judiciary, special-interest groups, the political party organizations, and the media of mass communication. The motivations and interests of these persons and groups may reflect rival opinions as to what is in the national interest, as well as rival personal or special interests and opinions that have little or nothing to do with the national interest. The influences brought to bear are so diverse, the participation can be so broad, and the process of making decisions for the United States in foreign affairs is so complex, that it is not always easy even for Americans to understand why a particular decision was reached by the American government. If that is true of the country in which we live and which we presumably understand the best, it is all the more true of foreign countries, especially closed societies, the workings of whose governments are concealed from us.

As a practical matter of intelligence-gathering about foreign countries, these difficulties are compounded by the problem of trying to understand the thought processes and the political processes at work in a society that is foreign to the observer. Soviet specialists in American affairs demonstrate in their writings that, despite an impressive grasp of the factual material, their Marxist analysis of how our governmental system functions is so beside the point that they miss the essence of our politics. Perhaps those who inhabit the Kremlin find the writings of our Kremlinologists to be equally beside the point. An accurate knowledge of the facts, though valuable, is not enough. Thus the Israeli intelligence services were fully aware of what the Egyptians were doing immediately before the outbreak of the Yom Kippur War of 1973, but failed to anticipate the Egyptian attack because they misunderstood the thinking of the Egyptian leaders and therefore misinterpreted the data.

Another difficulty in analyzing the thought processes of certain foreign leadership groups is that we can see that they do not follow the dictates of the philosophy that they profess, but we cannot be sure that they see this as clearly as we do. If the military dictator of an African or Latin American nation describes his regime as Marxist, even though objectively speaking it is no different from neighboring military dictatorships without ideological pretensions, does he in fact believe his own claims, and, if so, does his belief affect his actions in any way? It is a question that has to be answered in the circumstance of the particular case. It is an important question and on a much more sophisticated level, it has to be asked anew about that uncommunist and unproletarian dictatorship, the government of the Soviet Union, whenever a shift in power within the ruling group suggests that there has been a change in regime. Does the government of the Soviet Union reserve its Marxism exclusively for use in analyzing the structure of politics within the United States? Have there been any regimes, in the long history of the Soviet Union, that have recognized that their personal or oligarchic dictatorships bear little relationship to the working class government described by Marx; and, if so, has it affected either their decisions or the confidence with which they have carried out their decisions? Only the analysis of a specific Soviet leadership group can supply the answer.

As has been seen, there are many important things that can be known only by making a study, in its own unique terms, of one individual government at a given time in its history. But there is a good deal to be learned, too, by an analysis of the processes and structures that are common to a number of contemporary national governments. Professor Herbert Simon, who won the Nobel Prize for economics in 1978, has provided a set of concepts and a vocabulary suitable for describing the way an administrative organization actually works in the real world; studies of governmental organization might similarly analyze the decisions taken by bureaucracies in countries having roughly similar bureaucratic cultures, and for which the context is comparable.[3]

Only by studying the science of international relations in its own terms—the terms of independence and of states—can we make a start in applying the knowledge that is genuinely relevant. It is a good idea to take the waters, but we ought to do it at the right spa.

---

[3]Herbert A. Simon, *Administrative Behavior: A Study of Decision-Making Processes in Administrative Organization* (New York: The Macmillan Company, 1947).

4

A FALSE ANALOGY

The actual behavior of states toward one another, which ought to be the main subject matter of international relations, always has been ignored in the literature because students of the field have been in the grip of a powerful and misleading analogy: setting the mutual relations of the independent states of the world as equivalent to the mutual relations of individual fellow citizens of the same political commonwealth.[1] The misleading person-state analogy led to the muddles about power and morality discussed in Chapter 2, and to the mixup, discussed in Chapter 3, about the sciences that can be of help in understanding international relations. The same misleading analogy causes authorities in the field of international relations to discuss the ways in which conflicts are resolved in world politics as though they were the same as those commonly used in domestic politics.

---

[1]There are, of course, areas of similarity; indeed the analogy would not exert so powerful an attraction if there were not. But there are political differences between persons and states that are so profound that I think the analogy, useful though it sometimes is, ought to be used only with the greatest care. As it is, it frequently is abused, being used to suggest similarities where there are none.

They are not; they are, as I propose to show, fundamentally different.

. I am going to list and discuss a number of conflict-resolving compromises typical of world politics but not of domestic politics, compromises which, therefore, are ignored by scholars of international relations. I will discuss them not in complete detail but thoroughly enough to show that it is not because there is little to say about them that they are ignored; I will show with a number of examples, instead, that ignoring one or another type of compromise is not an isolated coincidence, but rather a part of a pattern of refusing to recognize the special realities of international relations.

In international relations, there is a question that has no real parallel in interpersonal relations: which groups are entitled to be independent states? Nobody can doubt that a human being is an entity, but whether a particular cluster of persons legitimately constitutes an entity is an open question, and a question of the utmost political significance. The struggle to achieve and maintain individual identity is therefore a characteristic and unique feature of international politics. For the past ten or fifteen thousand years, this struggle has had the special attribute that it is inextricably bound up with the struggle for territory. In a nomad world it might be otherwise, but our states are territorial and settled, and, by and large, all of the world's habitable area is claimed by the existing nations. National claims are jealously exclusive; many of the cruelest acts in political history have been directed against persons accused of forming a nation within a nation. A group, in order to achieve its nationhood, therefore lays a territorial claim that is exclusive; and, since oftentimes the same territory is also claimed by others, the assertion of nationhood throws down the gauntlet. Ever since civilization began, the human race has been at war to determine which group should occupy which space.

The extent, value, and military advantage of a nation's territory are of the essence of its life as a nation; maintenance or acquisition of the territory is rightly spoken of in terms of interests that are vital. The situation is far different for an individual, for whom the owning of property is desirable but not essential; I can be a free man — some would say a freer man — without owning anything. Thus the question of property assumes dimensions in international politics that it does not possess in domestic life and politics.

Typically, in a country such as our own, if a person believes he is entitled to land that is occupied by somebody else, he sues at law for the possession of it. If a person wants to acquire land that is owned by someone else, he offers to buy it. Analogizing such private transactions to international relations, international lawyers have written whole libraries of books outlining the application of the same procedures to the real estate affairs of nations.

It is true that there are a few isolated examples of the acquisition of national territory by purchase; the Louisiana and Alaska purchases are among the more spectacular ones. But these are rare and unusual events. Nations hardly ever part with land for money,[2] though individuals do it all the time. Money means much less to nations than it does to individuals, and land means much more. To an individual, land is merely a material possession; to a nation, territory is life itself. Therefore, nations rarely settle their important territorial conflicts through such procedures.

War, and the conquest by one side of the other, is the usual way of dealing with these matters in international relations. But, because of the independence of states, conquests often are not final solutions. As long as the defeated nation survives a territorial loss, or, as a people and culture, the loss of independence itself, the settlement remains impermanent. The ghosts of lost causes

------

[2]Sovereign rulers used to trade and purchase territories more freely than nations now do precisely because the rulers were in a position akin to private landholders. Sovereign princes used to regard the countries they ruled as private estates rather than public ones.

43

haunt the world of international affairs; they do not disappear for a very long time, if at all. General James Wolfe took Quebec from the French in 1759 in a victory over the Marquis de Montcalm that was thought to be decisive; but more than two centuries later, the leaders of French Quebec propose to rescind that victory. Elsewhere, too, the past is alive; the banners of yesterday fly over much of Eurasia and Africa. The Basques still are in arms. The cause of Greater Somalia has been revived. The soldiers of Kurdistan still take the field in pursuit of the statehood that always has been withheld from them. Judaea has returned to life two thousand years after being destroyed. Underground radio stations assert the claims of the Celtic peoples to European lands that they dominated in the first millennium B.C.

Conquests, then, are unstable; and the less sweeping solutions to international disputes are much more so. An analysis of typical compromises in international relations such as spheres of influence, neutralization, buffer zones, population exchange, and partition demonstrates the unsatisfactory, unsettled, and unsettling characteristics of solutions to international problems as contrasted with those available in domestic politics. Yet the point is that, for better or for worse, these are the only solutions that are available in an international arena, where the contestants are independent. Such as they are, here are some solutions typical of international politics.

Spheres and Zones

Spheres of influence can be established by mutual agreement between rival Powers; it is especially easy to do so when the Powers are geographically remote from one another. Each gains a free hand within its own sphere and concedes a free hand to its rival within its rival's sphere. It can be argued that the Helsinki accords of 1975 represent such an agreement between the U.S. and the U.S.S.R. with respect to the European continent.

Spheres of influence also can emerge in the course of events; or they can be asserted unilaterally. The United States made such an assertion with respect to Latin America by promulgation of the Monroe Doctrine. The effect and meaning of that unilateral assertion are now being tested anew by the continuing Russian presence in Cuba.

The converse of an agreement to give one another a free hand is neutralization by an agreement that neither Power will act. Thus Russian and British differences over Tibet were resolved in 1907 by an agreement that neither Power would send diplomatic representatives to the Tibetan capital at Lhasa. Similarly it was British policy in the nineteenth century to associate several European Powers in demands made upon the Ottoman empire, so that the ambitions of each Power would be restrained by the ambitions of the others.

Another type of agreement aimed at taking the edge off rival ambitions is that which results in the creation or maintenance of buffer states or buffer zones between the Powers. The late Professor Martin Wight,[3] one of the rare and enlightening scholars who dealt with these issues, classified buffer states as trimmers, neutrals, or satellites, depending upon the policy that they pursue.[4] Presumably another system of classification could be established in terms of the policies pursued by the Powers towards the buffers rather than vice versa.

Buffer states and zones often have been regarded as vital to the stability of international relations. Great importance has been attached to their existence: Powers have gone to war in order to defend buffer states, as Great Britain did in 1914 in response to the invasion of Belgium. On the other hand there are those who doubt the value of buffer areas. Bismarck's views on the proposed partition of the Ottoman empire suggest that he may have been among these. A. J. P. Taylor, in a footnote to his monumental

---

[3]One of the many great services perfomed by Professor Hedley Bull is that he has brought the works of Martin Wight to the attention of a wider public.

[4]Wight, *Power Politics*, p. 160.

study of nineteenth-century European diplomacy, outlined the divergent views in sentences that indicate the difficulty of forming a judgment:

> But did Bismarck really believe that partition made for lasting peace between the partitioning Powers? It is impossible to say. The partition of Poland perhaps drew Russia, Prussia, and Austria together, though not always. Other examples — such as the partition of Persia between Russia and Great Britain in 1907; of the Levant between Great Britain and France after 1919; or of Poland and the Near East between Russia and Germany in 1939 — are less encouraging. It is not an unreasonable generalization that the Anglo-Saxons and perhaps the French believe in buffer states and the Germans and perhaps the Russians believe in partition as the best way to peace between the Great Powers.[5]

This was one of the great issues of nineteenth-century international politics. A chief concern of Great Britain at that time was to preserve the integrity of the Ottoman empire against the encroachments of the other Great Powers, in part because the Ottoman empire served as a buffer between Britain-in-Asia and the advancing Russians.[6] But propping up the Ottoman regime seemed doomed to failure in the long run. A flaw in the policy of establishing buffer states is that if a state is weak enough to serve as a buffer, it may be too weak to stand on its own feet; its sponsors then will be obliged to try to rescue it — perhaps, in the end, without success.

On the other hand, successive British governments feared that a partition of Ottoman Asia would prove dangerous because an explosive situation is created when the armies of rival Powers come into direct contact. The tensions aroused by divided Berlin since the end of the Second World War suggest that British fears in this respect may not have been exaggerated.

---

[5]A. J. P. Taylor, *The Struggle for Mastery in Europe, 1848-1914* (Oxford: At the Clarendon Press, 1954), p. 239, note 1.

[6]David Fromkin, "The Great Game in Asia," *Foreign Affairs* 58 (Spring 1980), pp. 936-951.

Similar considerations came into play in the case of China at the turn of the century, as rival Powers sought spheres of influence and perhaps partition. In 1899–1900 U.S. Secretary of State John Hay proposed a contrary policy, in which there would be an "Open Door" for all into a China whose territorial integrity would be preserved. His proposal reflected the view that the establishment of China as a buffer state was much to be preferred to the partition of China by colonialist Powers.

Contrary views about buffers, neutralizations, and partitions have been evidenced since 1945 in the discussions about whether the Russian and American presences in Europe should be separated, and if so, in what manner; and whether there should be mutual troop withdrawals, or an area free of nuclear weapons, or some combination of various of these approaches. But in the literature of international relations, I have never yet encountered a book about buffer states. Perhaps one exists, but there can hardly be many of them — and the subject is of genuine importance in the real world that the literature of international relations is supposed to describe.

Exodus

International conflicts often result in the uprooting of populations. This is particularly true in conflicts that result in partition, where a transfer of populations can be seen as the logical completion of the partition. Such was the case with the movement of national minorities in the course of the Balkan and Greco-Turkish wars between 1912 and 1922.[7] No fewer than seventeen migratory movements took place in Macedonia alone in the years that began with the First Balkan War (1912).[8] But it was not until

---

[7]Stephen P. Ladas, *The Exchange of Minorities: Bulgaria, Greece and Turkey* (New York: The Macmillan Company, 1932), p. 1.

[8]Ladas, *Minorities,* p. 15

the final population movements arising from these wars at the end of the 1922 campaign that the mass expulsion of minorities came to be seen not as an international problem but as an international solution.

After Turkey defeated Greece in the campaign of 1922, an outstanding issue between the two countries was the fate of the roughly 1.3 million Greeks who had fled or been expelled from Turkey. Turkey refused to allow them to return. On December 1, 1922, Dr. Fridtjof Nansen, the Norwegian statesman and winner of the Nobel Peace Prize, declared that a mass flight of refugees of such epic dimensions was not reversible; and he proposed that the exodus be treated a a *fait accompli* that could provide the basis for a mutual population transfer. Dr. Nansen's suggestion was accepted; and pursuant to the ensuing agreement, Greece expelled 400,000 Turks.[9]

The agreement between Greece and Turkey, and an earlier one between Greece and Bulgaria, pursuant to which 250,000 Bulgarians left Greek territory, regulated the treatment of emigrants and of their assets. These agreements dealt with such questions as taxes, customs duties, the appraisal of real estate and other assets left behind, the terms of the bonds which might be given in payment for such assets and the guarantees securing such bonds, the transfer of funds, the disposal of mining, fishing, and other intangible rights, the disposal of community property, and the payment to be made for transportation out of the country.

These legal and diplomatic agreements were attempts to ameliorate the harsh human consequences of the uprooting of populations. As such they deserved the applause that they received. But an unfortunate consequence of such success as they achieved was that they lent a certain respectability to the expulsion of populations. The very name that was used to describe what had happened — "the exchange of minorities" — was a cosmetic.

---

[9]Ladas, *Minorities,* pp. 446–447; L. S. Stavrianos, *The Balkans Since 1453* (New York: Rinehart & Company, Inc., 1958), p. 11.

An exchange suggests a transaction that is somewhat fair, because there is a give-and-take. It suggests, too, a voluntary transaction, in which each party gives and gets what it chooses. The name gives no hint of the anguish and suffering that are its reality. Years later, writing of these Greek-Bulgarian-Turkish matters, the editors of *Foreign Affairs* gave it as their opinion that, "while such exchanges of minorities may indeed permanently resolve past discords, it would be a rash or callous statesman who would urge population transfers as a solution: the human costs were tremendous."[10]

At the time, of course, it was thought that these events in the Balkans and in Asia Minor, though terrible, constituted an isolated episode in modern history. On the contrary, they proved to be merely the first in a series of brutal displacements of whole populations characteristic of international relations in the twentieth century. Among these were the population transfers imposed by Stalin on the Baltic states in 1939-40, the transfer of Karelian Finns to Finland and the Sudeten Germans to Germany, after the Second World War, and, at about the same time, the transfers of millions of people between the Soviet Union and Poland and Czechoslovakia, and between Hungary and her neighbors. In the wake of the partition of India and the creation of Pakistan, minority populations of nearly 15 million people fled from one to the other, and hundreds of thousands died along the way.[11] Reliable figures are hard to come by, but one expert has estimated that during the period from 1913 to 1968 minority exchange and refugee populations totalled 71.1 million.[12] A higher figure is suggested by the statement of Israeli Foreign Minister Moshe Sharrett in 1950 that, at that time alone and in what he

---

[10]Dexter, ed., *50-Year Bibliography*, p. 631.

[11]*Encyclopaedia Britannica*, 15th Ed., s.v. "Indian Subcontinent, History of the."

[12]Kingsley Davis, "The Migration of Human Populations," *Scientific American*, Vol. 231 (September 1974), pp. 92, 102.

regarded as the Free World, there were 60 million refugees.[13]

Especially terrible is the plight of those forced to leave the country of their birth who have no other place to go. Armenians fleeing the massacres of their people by the Turks, a million White Russians fleeing the Bolsheviks, and Jews fleeing the Nazis had no state of their own to give them sanctuary; and the other states were reluctant to let them enter.

The justification for expelling minorities is thought to be the perfection of national independence. Throwing off the foreign yoke is not enough; the exercise of its independence requires a nation to obtain exclusive possession of its territory. The massacres of Armenians, the burning of Smyrna, and the expulsion of more than a million Greek and other Christians as a result of the Turkish victory of 1922 are often described as a successful solution to Turkey's minorities problem. Moreover the refugees who flooded into Greece are said to have enriched the life of that country. The great Liberal historian H. A. L. Fisher, who expressed this point of view, dispassionately concluded his account of these terrible events by writing: "Thus did the principle of self-determination work itself out through fire and sword in the half-savage East."[14]

But what if the tragedies and the suffering occur, and yet no solution results from it? That is one of the novel problems that the Arab-Israeli wars have introduced into international relations. After the 1948 war in which Israel gained her independence, Jewish communities in many Islamic countries left, fled, or were forced to flee, to Israel. These included more than 120,000 Jews from Iraq, 50,000 from Yemen and Aden, nearly 40,000 from Iran, more than 30,000 from Turkey, 160,000 from North Africa, and tens of thousands of others from Libya, Egypt, Syria,

---

[13]Howard M. Sachar, *A History of Israel: From the Rise of Zionism to Our Time* (New York: Alfred A. Knopf, 1976), p. 440.

[14]H. A. L. Fisher, *A History of Europe: From The Beginning of the 18th Century to 1937* (London: Eyre & Spottiswoode, 1952), p. 1181.

Lebanon, and elsewhere.[15] In all this amounted to more than 400,000 Jewish refugees from Arab and Islamic countries; but the Israelis made the necessary effort and settled them and integrated them into the country. But the more than 500,000 Arabs who fled from Israel were not integrated into many of the Arab countries in which they sought refuge. Their integration would have meant an acceptance of a *fait accompli,* such as Nansen had recommended to Greece in 1922; and the Arab governments were determined not to accept it. Masses of Arab refugees were kept in special camps in Egyptian Gaza, in Lebanon, and elsewhere; and there, for three decades, families have lived and died, in poverty and squalor, without hope or home. The festering hatred and the nihilistic terrorism that this has engendered have indeed kept the results of the war of 1948, including the establishment of the state of Israel, from being accepted by the Arab world. Thus the policy, at an enormous cost in terms of human suffering, has been a political success for Arab governments.[16]

Will this refusal to accept an exchange of populations be an example that other nations will follow in the future? Will this make partition an even less viable solution to territorial conflicts? The implications of the Arab policy on refugees have not been adequately examined because the Arab refugee question, like so many other refugee questions that have arisen, is thought of as an isolated and one-time thing. What is not widely enough understood is that the refugee question is a permanent one, and that it constitutes a continuing feature of the way in which international politics function in the twentieth century.

Thus the exodus from Indochina that began in 1975 and made headline news in 1979 took the world by surprise. In 1979

---

[15]Sachar, *Israel,* pp. 395 et seq.

[16]A success, that is, in the sense that it accomplished the objective it was intended to accomplish. In a wider sense it may not be a success, because the Arab governments no longer can control the forces that they long ago unleashed.

the Vietnamese government indicated that it intended to expel all of its subjects who were of ethnic Chinese origin—a group numbering about 1 or 1.5 million people.[17] It was an unexpected decision because when a twentieth-century government decides to purge its country completely of a hated minority, observers persuade themselves and others that it is an act of cruelty that is unique, and that the world has become too civilized to allow such a thing ever to happen again. In the case of the ethnic Chinese, comfort also could be taken from the expectation that their ancestral homeland would accept and care for them. But there was a flow of non-Chinese refugees as well, with nowhere to go; and though the U.S. took the lead in offering refuge to many of them, the world was dismayingly slow to grasp the nature and dimensions of the crisis. When the government of Malaysia announced that it would drive the refugees out to sea, and would shoot any refugees who tried to come ashore, it shocked a number of other governments into saying that they would do something.[18] Yet not very much was done.

It is evident that the governments of the world were not prepared to deal with a problem of this sort and of this size. According to a news report that was published in the summer of 1979, the United Nations High Commissioner for Refugees was too short of funds to carry out his aid programs for the Indochinese: in Hong Kong the High Commissioner's office had to cut off the $1.20 daily food allowance that it had provided for unemployed refugees, and in Bangkok the High Commissioner could afford to supply only a few dozen employees to deal with 16 refugee camps and 175,000 refugees.[19] Although at that time half a million refugees drowned in the South China Sea while trying to escape, and a million living refugees had come out of Indochina, and three million more were expected to come, and—at the end of June 1979—it was predicted that 100,000 refugees

---

[17]New York *Times*, June 12, 1979, p. 1.
[18]International *Herald Tribune*, June 16–17, 1979, p. 1.
[19]*Time*, August 13, 1979, p. 14.

would die within the following six weeks alone, the governments of the world had no solution to offer.[20] The humane governments said they were sorry, while the government of the Soviet Union said that the Indochinese refugee problem was merely a figment of the capitalist press.[21]

It began to be clear that Vietnam had discovered yet another way in which to make political use of refugees. By expelling hordes of refugees into neighboring countries whose economic and social fabric was fragile, Vietnam used a weapon that those neighbors soon recognized was deadly. There were all the makings of successful blackmail. Neighboring countries had a strong incentive to meet Vietnam's terms lest she expel more of her population. Vietnam had invented a way to profit from creating a refugee problem. Other states are bound to emulate her.

The boat people of Indochina — a people without a country, doomed to drift at sea until they die, because no country in the vicinity will let them in — are a haunting and eerie image of the real international politics of the twentieth century. Africa, the Balkans, and most of all, Asia, are intermixed with thousands of ethnic, tribal, linguistic, and religious varieties of people; and the heartless demands of majoritarian purity seem likely to continue to drive out masses of them as refugees for as many years ahead as we can see. It is at best a terrible solution, and at worst no solution at all, but world politics provide no alternative.

Wars and invasions, the traditional causes of mass population flights, will continue to drive out refugees, too. At the end of 1980, there already were a million refugees from Ethiopia in Somalia.[22] In the spring of 1981, the New York *Times* reported of Africa in general that "The number of refugees keeps rising as Africans battle Africans," and added that "The number of

---

[20]*The Economist*, July 21, 1979, pp. 11-12.

[21]Ibid.

[22]Somalia: New York *Times*, November 6, 1980, p. A-11. Africa in general: New York *Times*, April 7, 1981, p. A-2.

refugees has risen sharply in recent years, from one million in 1975 to five million today." In 1981, too, a Reuters dispatch from Asia indicated that a million refugees from Afghanistan, mostly women and children, had arrived in Pakistan in the twelve months after the Soviet Union had invaded Afghanistan in December 1979.[23]

It is a general and continuing problem. It arises from the independence of states, which gives each government the freedom to choose who may and who may not enter and reside in the country it governs. Because there is no political structure for the world as a whole, there is no place in the world that is obliged to give sanctuary to the outcasts.

Here, then, is an important and ignored problem of the world politics of our time. It is beginning at last to receive some attention in the field of international law, in the rapidly developing law of international refugees. For the most part, the literature of international relations, however, treats it as though it did not exist as a general problem: it is pictured as a few tragic episodes that are unlikely to recur. The classic study of whole populations that are driven out of their countries asserts that "These uprootings of populations occurred in relatively unenlightened periods of history when respect for the rights of man was hardly recognized, either in international or in national law."[24] The study appeared nearly a half-century ago and claimed that what Turkey and Greece had done at that time in driving out their minority populations was unique; the world had become too civilized for minority populations ever to be uprooted and driven out again.[25]

Partition

Partition is another important political expedient that is typical of international relations and that is ignored in the literature. Yet an

---

[23]International *Herald Tribune*, January 5, 1981, p. 2.
[24]Ladas, *Minorities*, p. 1.
[25]Ladas, *Minorities*, p. 2.

appreciation of its characteristics is essential to an understanding of the international politics of the modern world.

The key to an understanding of the dynamics of partition is the observation that, while partitions may be accepted, they are rarely desired. It is a fair generalization that most conflicts involve at least one party who wants to win the whole territory at stake. Even if obliged to take whatever they can get now, at least some of the parties often do so with the thought of getting the rest later. Partitions tend to be unstable when they are regarded for this reason as provisional.

They also are unstable because they are unjust. If a judge were to force parties to share the possession of some disputed property, presumably he would do so on the basis of his notion, however misconceived, of justice or equity. But the partitions of territories in international relations, as well as the terms and conditions of the partitions, result from power factors rather than from anybody's notion of what is right. Literally, or figuratively, the line of partition is drawn wherever the rival armies happen to meet.

For evident reasons, partition is resented most keenly by the inhabitants of the territory in dispute. "No country in the world likes to be partitioned," as King Hussein of Jordan once wrote.[26] Thus dividing a country between the rival indigenous nations that claim it as their homeland is the most unstable type of partition, for such parties never regard it as a just solution. They may accept it temporarily, if circumstances force them to do so; but in the typical case, they will plan to overthrow the settlement by force of arms as soon as they think themselves able to do so.

When two or more countries, however, agree to divide between themselves a territory that is *foreign* to all of them, what results is the type of partition that is the least unstable. Indeed,

---

[26]King Abdallah of Jordan, *My Memoirs Completed: "Al Takmilah,"* tr. Harold W. Glidden (London and New York: Longman, 1978), p. xvi. The reference is to the Foreword by King Hussein.

their partnership in partition may, under certain political circumstances, bring the occupying Powers into a sort of alliance. Martin Wight observed that

> When powers become adjacent through partitioning a territory to which their right is challenged, this challenge will tend to make them interdependent. Prussia and Russia established a common frontier by the Partition of Poland at the end of the eighteenth century, and a joint interest in suppressing Polish nationalism was the basis of their friendship for more than a hundred years. After the First World War Soviet Russia and Nationalist Turkey cooperated to eliminate the Transcaucasian republics that had sprung up between them when the Russian and Ottoman Empires collapsed, and this was an element (though weak in proportion to the weakness of Transcaucasian nationalism) in the good relations between Russia and Turkey between the wars. Israel and Jordan partitioned Jerusalem in 1948 in defiance of a United Nations resolution establishing it as a Free City, and partly for this reason Israeli-Jordanian relations have been less exacerbated than Israel's relations with the other Arab powers. Turkey, Iraq and Persia have a common interest in the partitioning of the Kurdish people, which will grow as Kurdish nationalism grows.[27]

One of the great political dramas of the twentieth century is the disintegration of European colonial empires. Here too the significance of partition, and also of the proposal of partition, ought not to be overlooked. Often, for example when partition is proposed or administered by a colonial Power in the country that it occupies, its function is to divide the loyalties of the peoples of the subject country in order to weaken their resistance to colonial rule. A complementary strategy is the proposal of partition by a minority group within a colony on the verge of independence, in an effort either to block the granting of independence or else to modify the terms under which the majority would assume power after independence is attained. Like King Solomon, the minority may propose a cutting in two without seriously intending it to happen, intending rather that the threat of so unacceptable a

---

[27]Wight, *Power Politics*, pp. 157–158.

solution will force either the colonial Power or the majority to pay a price for the withdrawal of the proposal.

It might have been in pursuit of this strategy that Sir Edward Carson, the opponent of Home Rule for Ireland, repeatedly proposed from 1910 onward that northern Ireland should split away from southern Ireland if Home Rule were granted, for his hope had been to keep all of Ireland under British rule forever. Perhaps there was an element of calculation, too, in the proposal by another brilliant British barrister, Mohammed Ali Jinnah, of an independent Moslem state to be called Pakistan, when the Congress party refused to share the leadership of India with his Muslim League. If so, the breakup of India was the result of a failure by the other Congress party leaders to follow Mahatma Gandhi along the path of making concessions to Jinnah.

History is filled with stories of partition: of countries, such as much-partitioned Poland; of empires, such as Rome, divided between the Latin west and the Greek east; of continents, such as Africa in the colonializing nineteenth century; of the vast unknown, as when Spain and Portugal, in 1493–94, partitioned all the rest of the world that their navigators and explorers might find.

Recent history, at least for the United States, has been dominated by the consequences of partitions, and by the fact that partitions are unstable because they are not grounded in reason or consent. Wars broke out in partitioned Korea and in partitioned Vietnam; and American support of the status-quo partition lines brought the United States into its two post-1945 wars, the one to preserve the partition of Korea, the other to preserve the partition of Vietnam. In the Indian subcontinent, however, the U.S. joined China in opposing partition, but failed to prevent India from effecting the political partition of Pakistan into its eastern and western parts.

Current concerns, too, focus on partitions, especially in Europe, where the fate of partitioned Germany remains a central issue in world politics, and in the Middle East, where the proposed and contested partitions of Palestine[28] and Lebanon continue to threaten and disrupt the peace of the world.

Ever since the end of the Second World War, the partition of Europe into Soviet and non-Soviet spheres has seemed to be the major issue in global politics. Europe was the principal theatre of the Cold War between the U.S. and the U.S.S.R. America refused to accept as permanent the Russian control of eastern Europe; and Russian-inspired communist parties undermined the stability of western European governments allied with the United States. But Secretary of State Dulles, though the advocate of liberating eastern Europe, failed to come to the aid of revolutions in east Berlin and Hungary; the U.S. did not oppose the invasion of Czechoslovakia by Russia and her Warsaw Pact allies; and a few years back, at Helsinki, the United States appeared to relinquish its claims contesting the Soviet domination of eastern Europe. Many proclaimed that the Cold War had ended.

Indeed a member of the Policy Planning Staff of the U.S. Department of State has recently written an elegant book persuasively arguing that the division of Europe is neither unstable nor transitory, that it serves the interests of the Powers that matter and, therefore, that it will endure.[29]

---

[28]Palestine resulted from the partition of the Ottoman empire and of Syria at the end of the First World War, for Palestine until then had been southern Syria. In 1922, Palestine was further partitioned under the terms of the British White Paper of that year into western Palestine, where a Jewish National Home was to be developed, and eastern Palestine, called Transjordan and later Jordan, which was to remain exclusively Arab. In 1947, the United Nations proposed a further partition of western Palestine into Jewish and Arab sections, with an international status for Jerusalem. The 1948 war between Jews and Arabs resulted in a partition of western Palestine between the new Jewish State of Israel and the new east Palestinian State of Jordan, along lines not identical with those proposed by the United Nations. In the 1967 war, Israel occupied all of western Palestine, and since then has resisted efforts to once again partition it.

[29]A. W. DePorte, *Europe Between the Superpowers: The Enduring Balance* (New Haven and London: Yale University Press, 1979).

Yet, at the heart of divided Europe lies partitioned Germany; and Germany's future is still at issue. Germany's fate was, one could argue, the essential issue about which the Cold War was waged. It was and is a dangerous issue, because the stakes are so high. Reunification of Germany is an issue that arouses emotion, and German nationalism is far from dormant. There is a risk that some future German government might be swept along by a tide of emotion into taking action. An attempt by either west or east Germans to reunify their country by force of arms would imperil the rest of us. In the circumstances of the twentieth century, the third German war might lead to the end of the world.

If a new world war occurs, its occasion, therefore, or at least its excuse, is likely to be a contested partition. If not Germany, then Palestine; and if not Palestine, then another. A Russian descent on Iran could move through partitioned Azerbaijan, and might masquerade as support for a united Azerbaijan. A Russian attack on China might take place through partitioned Turkestan, and might masquerade as support for a revolt in eastern Turkestan against Chinese rule and in favor of a reunited Turkestan.

The Head in the Sand

Partition and the expulsion of populations, like conquest, neutralization, and the establishment of buffer states or spheres of influence, are expedients characteristic of international relations. Adjudication and arbitration, on the contrary, are processes characteristic of domestic affairs. Yet, carried away by the person-state analogy, writers in the field of international relations have devoted an inordinate amount of space and attention to the latter processes, the ones that play no significant role in the settlement of the great issues in world politics. Writers and academics are not the only ones who commit this error. Governments, too, devote a disproportionate amount of time and effort to these juristic matters.

George Kennan, whose diplomatic career began half a century ago, wrote wisely and sadly of the emptiness of this legalistic program for dealing with world affairs:

> The United States Government, during the period from the turn of the century to the 1930s, signed and ratified a total of ninety-seven international agreements dealing with arbitration or conciliation, and negotiated a number of others which, for one reason or another, never took effect. Of the ninety-seven, seven were multilateral ones; the remainder, bilateral. The time, trouble, and correspondence that went into the negotiation of this great body of contractual material was stupendous. Yet so far as I can ascertain, only two of these treaties or conventions were ever invoked in any way. Only two disputes were actually arbitrated on the basis of any of these instruments; and there is no reason to suppose that these disputes would not have been arbitrated anyway, on the basis of special agreements, had the general treaties not existed. The other ninety-five treaties, including incidentally every single one negotiated by Secretaries of State Bryan, Kellogg and Stimson, appear to have remained wholly barren of any practical result. Nor is there any evidence that this ant-like labor had the faintest effect on the development of the terrible wars and upheavals by which the first half of this century was marked.[30]

The proportions are all wrong. Too much effort is devoted to matters that in international affairs are not of great consequence. Too many books are written about subjects that are in large part irrelevant or inconsequential, while too few studies are undertaken of the subjects that are at the heart of world politics. The study of international relations needs a new syllabus.

The Library of Congress contains nearly 600 titles of books pertaining to the settlement of international disputes by courts or arbitral tribunals; many of these are multi-volume sets. Yet adjudication and arbitration, as the recollection of George Kennan indicates, are of little, if any, importance in the real world of international conflicts.

---

[30]George F. Kennan, *Realities of American Foreign Policy* (Princeton: Princeton University Press, 1954), pp. 18-19.

In 1972, when I was working on foreign policy problems for Hubert Humphrey, I happened to look into the general subject of partition, its nature, characteristics, and dynamics. Partition was the issue in Korea and Vietnam, and is the issue in Europe, in Germany, and in Palestine. Partition is the issue of the Cold War, and was the issue of both of America's hot wars after 1945. Partition is the explosively unstable type of solution that in Europe or the Middle East could bring about the Third World War, which would likely mean the end of the world. In searching, I found that there were no books, in any language, on the general subject of partition.[31]

That, then, is evidence for the proposition that we have not been told about the real world and about what goes on in it. This in turn may in part be responsible for what we will now see: that even political leaders often do not understand what goes on in the real world of international politics.

---

[31]The situation is little better today. Thus it is only the Introduction of Ray Edward Johnston, ed., *The Politics of Division, Partition, and Unification* (New York: Praeger Publishers, 1976) that deals with partition in general; the chapters themselves, in this slender volume, deal with the issues raised by specific partitions. This short anthology, and an out-of-print volume by Thomas E. Hachey, one of the authors represented in it, are the only additions to the literature indicated by the card-index in the Library of Congress from 1972 to date.

5

THE IRONIES OF INTERNATIONAL RELATIONS

Until now this book has been concerned, for the most part, with the consequences in theory of recognizing or failing to recognize the difference between international and domestic politics. But there are practical consequences too, both for those who govern and for their opponents.

Stanley Baldwin was the greatest House of Commons politician of his time. Lyndon Johnson, as majority leader in the Senate, seemed to be the shrewdest politician in the country. But both men, when in power, pursued foreign policies that proved disastrous. It is typical, rather than paradoxical, that men skilled in domestic politics were unskilled in foreign affairs. Conversely, it is not unusual for great ambassadors and foreign ministers to misunderstand the politics of their own countries.

Knowing how to deal with one's own group is different from knowing how to deal with outside groups; and knowing how to deal within a political and legal structure is different from knowing how to deal with independent entities outside the framework of any structure. Abilities in the one realm of endeavor do not necessarily carry over into the other. Those who try to do in world politics what they do in domestic politics find themselves in something like a carnival house of tricks, in which every movement leads to unexpected results. They find themselves engaged in the unfamiliar politics of an upside-down world, in which their actions often have consequences that they did not intend, sometimes the direct opposite of those that they had intended. For them, the world of international relations is a strange land of unexpected ironies.

The Fifth Column

One of the oldest arguments in political history concerns whether or not a person should give his highest loyalty to the state. From earliest times, men of religion have asserted that the claims of God ought to come first; and, at least from the time of Socrates, philosophers have asserted that the claims of private conscience should be put first. In everyday life, where concerns and attachments are down-to-earth, it is not unusual to find persons whose chief loyalty is to a tribe, a caste, a family, a church, a military organization, a social or economic class, or a political movement. These groups, organizations, and forces provide an alternative focal point for loyalties to which it is *practicable* to subordinate one's loyalties to the state.

Similar alternatives have existed at one time or another in transnational politics as a result of peculiar local circumstances. The most familiar example is that of medieval Europe, where supreme loyalty was to the church, where states in the modern sense did not exist, and where the power of the Pope overshadowed that of princes. Later, in the course of a long transition during which modern states emerged and the church declined, loyalties were torn and tested. Whether it was legitimate in the seventeenth century for French Protestants to seek aid from England, or in the sixteenth century for English Catholics to give aid to Spain, were, for a time, open questions. Now they are no longer open questions. One's country, however defined, comes first.[1] There are no groups, organizations, or forces in world politics that, in realistic terms, provide an alternative focal point for loyalties to which it would be practicable to subordinate one's loyalty to the state.

At the outset of the First World War, the proletarian Second International — the socialist organization that stood for the working class of the world in opposition to imperialist nationalism and its wars — broke apart in a frenzy of patriotic war fever; and its adherents rushed with enthusiasm to enlist under the standards of one or another of the rival nationalisms. The slogans of international working-class solidarity proved to be meaningless.

Generous visions that go beyond the frontiers of particular states are, in practice, again and again betrayed. When the armies of the French Revolution crossed into Italy in 1796-97, they did so under the banners of liberation and fraternity; but, like earlier enemies from abroad, they proved to be conquerors who looted and partitioned the country. The Italians who responded to the rhetoric of revolution were duped. It was a fraud; it was propaganda on behalf of the interests of the French state. The Directory that then governed France spoke in the language of democracy, but in a confidential answer to a request for policy guidance from its Foreign Minister in 1796, it responded:

"1st Question: Is it in the interest of the French Republic to instigate the formation of one or more democratic republics in the whole of Italy?"

"Answer: Decided in the negative."[2]

Posterity has tended to blame Bonaparte, as the French com-

---

[1]Oftentimes, in modern civil strife — in Northern Ireland, for example — the question of to which country one properly belongs is itself an issue.

[2]Guglielmo Ferrero, *The Gamble: Bonaparte in Italy, 1796-1797*, translated by Bertha Pritchard and Lily C. Freeman (New York: Walker and Company, 1961), pp. 96–97.

mander, for what occurred in Italy, but he was no more than carrying out the orders of his government. The failure to honor the promises made by the French revolutionaries was not a default that was personal. It was an illustration of the truth that in the modern world of sovereign states, ideologies are used in the service of states, and not the other way round. It was one of the first acts of political modernism. For this and other reasons, a leading twentieth-century historian has seen Bonaparte's Italian war as the turning point of European history.[3]

This drama often has been replayed. The story of the Ukrainians who welcomed the German armies as liberators from Stalin's Russia, only to be treated with Nazi ruthlessness, is a familiar one. Prince Sihanouk and his followers in Cambodia in 1979 were perhaps unique in opposing the forces (Vietnamese) that liberated them from a murderous tyranny on the realistic grounds that the forces were alien ones.

Sometimes supporting the forces of another country is the right thing to do. Willy Brandt, a German patriot, fought against his country in the Second World War because defeating Germany was the only way to destroy the Nazi threat to civilization. It was an exceptional case because the Norwegian leaders alongside whose forces Brandt fought shared his moral concerns and objectives. In the more usual case, the moral issue is merely made use of by governments to whom morality means little or nothing.

The international politics of the 1930s and early 1940s provide especially striking illustrations of the manipulation of ideologies to support the interests of states. These were years of poignant drama for political groups both of the right and left. The right and the left with equal wrong thought that the supreme political realities were transnational groups such as world capitalism and the world proletariat, whereas in reality such entities did not exist. Based upon such fantasies, significant right-wing elements of French society believed, for example, that Hitler was their friend

---

[3]Ferrero, *The Gamble.*

and Leon Blum was their enemy. Many of them pictured Hitler not as the leader of Germany, France's rival, but rather as the proponent of a New Order in Europe. There were idealists, and not merely opportunists, among those Frenchmen and other Europeans who collaborated with Nazi Germany. When their story came to an end in 1945, there were still some among them who believed that it was a European or global cause that they had served. Perhaps it would have been unbearable for them to face the harsh truth: that what they had served was not a cause, but an enemy state.

The tale of how left-wing groups at that time made a similar error is a familiar one. They thought that they were serving the cause of the working class or of world communism, when in fact all that they had been serving was the Russian national interest. It was not, of course, what most of them had intended; and many of them were never able to acknowledge the truth that what they had been supporting was not Marxism but the Soviet Union.

If either left or right had acted in the same sort of way, but within the context of domestic politics, they would have succeeded in supporting that which they had intended to support. In domestic politics, you can cast your lot with a particular political party or economic class because, on the *national* scale, these entities exist whereas on a *world* scale they do not. In international politics, power and loyalty are effectively organized only around states; so to support an ideology or movement that is not sponsored by a state is to enlist in a losing cause, while to support an ideology or movement that *is* sponsored by a particular state — no matter what your intentions — is to support the national interests of that state.

The Use of Force

Another of the basic issues in political science concerns the role of force in the making of political decisions. Civilized opinion op-

67

poses the primacy of force, and believes, instead, in due judicial, legislative, and administrative process. You and I, who hold these views, believe in the rule of reason. We believe in rule by consent rather than by coercion. We oppose the kind of government that seizes or maintains power through the use of police and armies, guns and tanks.

Most countries, it is true, *are* governed by military or police-state regimes. But they need not be. Constitutional regimes do exist in Western and northern Europe, in North America, in the Pacific, and, to some extent, elsewhere. Within the context of such constitutional regimes, it is feasible to oppose the use of force by one's own side because it is reasonable to suppose that the other side will not use force either, and that even if they wanted to, they would be effectively prevented from doing so by the armed services, the police, the business community, the trade unions, and other organized groups. Thus to be of the party that opposes the use of force is to adopt a point of view that is, at the very least, valid.

In international affairs, it is otherwise. States do use force when their governments feel the need or desire to do so, and there is no way they can be restrained from doing so other than by the use of countervailing force. Thus one cannot be of the party that opposes the use of force by states; one can only be of the party that opposes the use of force by one's own state, which is something quite different and leads to quite different results. The anti-fascist but pacifist British left-wing of the 1930s was obviously inconsistent, in that fascism only could be opposed successfully if anti-fascists gave up their pacifism; but even their pacifism itself contained a contradiction: because the British failure to rearm allowed Hitler and Mussolini to go from triumph to triumph, pacifism led to the success of militarism.

In France at that time, it was much the same. Charles de Gaulle preached in vain the need for a modern mechanized army to counter such threats as those posed by Nazi Germany. On June 7, 1940, just before the fall of France, the London *Times* described a series of lectures that de Gaulle had given at the Sorbonne and which had been heatedly interrupted. The *Times* explained the adverse reaction of the students by remarking that de Gaulle's ideas "appeared inconsistent with democracy to people who associated tanks with Nazism and Fascism."[4] They thought that they could vote against tanks. But they could only vote against French tanks — and by doing so they voted in favor of being ruled by tanks that were German.

Crusades

After the Crusades, and after the destruction of the Indian cultures of the New World, the wars of religion, both internal and among nations, in the sixteenth and seventeenth centuries in Europe brought home to the peoples of Europe how much suffering is caused when one group tries to force its religion upon another. A result of that terrible experience — the proof that the lesson had been learned — was the morally neutral character of foreign policies after the religious wars were brought to an end in 1648. France, which had been the first Christian country to establish diplomatic ties with the infidel Turk, in the modern world, too, has made rather a great point of not passing judgment on other countries or their governments. A similar, though not identical, point of view is suggested by the emphasis placed in diplomatic documents of the past few centuries, particularly those of the British Foreign Office, on the desirability of non-interference in the internal affairs of other countries. These traditions embody a hard-earned wisdom. Governments disregard it, as all too often they do nowadays, at their peril.

Of course, it is natural to want to extend the frontier of moral goals, and to seek the benefits of our values for the peoples of other countries. It goes against the grain to oppose a program that

---

[4]Major-General Sir Edward Spears, *Assignment to Catastrophe* (New York: A. A. Wyn, Inc., 1955). Vol. 2, *The Fall of France: June 1940*, p. 116.

seems so generous and that speaks so directly to the purposes for which politics ought to be pursued. Nobody ought to want to quarrel with the goal of doing good in the world, even though the definitions of doing good differ and often conflict. Pursuing policies that aim at realizing our moral values is the right thing to do in domestic politics; but the problem that arises when we try to do the same thing in foreign affairs comes from the fact that other nations are independent of us. There is a fundamental difference between living according to your own moral code and, on the other hand, forcing other peoples to live according to your moral code. There are both moral and practical dangers in trying to apply the moral principles of one nation to the rest of the world.

A practical difficulty is that it is expensive and risky. To some extent, all nations face dangers to their security and consequently need to ally themselves with other nations. It is suicidal to reject help from other nations because you disapprove of their morals, but to be selective in your morality, and only enforce your moral standards when it suits your interests to do so, is not morality but hypocrisy.

Another difficulty is that, although the members of a society tend to share or accept the same body of moral principles, nations differ from, and often oppose, one another in these matters. Thus one nation cannot always persuade another by an appeal to principles, as is done in domestic politics, for the principles are often not agreed upon; nor can one nation shame or inspire another by setting an example of carrying into practice a set of ideals if, in fact, such ideals are not shared. In the 1930s, the British government was unable to persuade Hitler and Mussolini not to intervene in the Spanish civil war because the Nazis and the Fascists had their own beliefs and objectives, which they thought would be better served by intervention; and Anthony Eden, we are told, was the only one in the British cabinet who came to understand it was futile to "set a good example" to Hitler and Mussolini.[5] Yet

---

[5]Elizabeth Wiskemann, *Europe of the Dictators: 1919-1945* (Glasgow: Fontana/Collins, 1966), p. 138.

the attempt was made, and the effect of the non-intervention example set by the western democracies was merely to let the enemies of democracy win by default, for the dictators did not follow the example. A British policy that was allegedly moral therefore led, in international affairs, to a result that, in terms of British ideals, was morally wrong.

The way in which a state that exercises restraint can influence another state to exercise similar restraint is through a tacit or express agreement that there will be reciprocity. But this is an appeal to mutual national interests, not to moral values. Even when countries do share the same system of values, it is not always helpful for one of them to try to induce another to carry those values into effect. National leaders and populations tend to be sensitive about their independence, and sometimes react to pressures or preachments from abroad, however well intentioned, in an angry and contrary sense. Telling other nations to do the right thing can persuade them to do the wrong thing. This is true even where nations are in basic agreement about principles, and is all the more true when they are not.

Another problem is that moral principles have to be *forced* on alien societies if they do not happen to share them. In domestic society, this is not true, for we share, if not common values, then at least a higher loyalty to our country and to its laws, which leads us to obey without having to be coerced into doing so. The lack of an overriding commitment to a common political order makes international politics different, and causes good-intentioned attempts to assert moral values to become bloody crusades that accomplish nothing but harm.

The attempt by a country to impose its own moral ideals on the rest of the world, if seriously undertaken, becomes a policy of war and conquest. The means invalidate the ends. Crusades may be intended to save the world, but in practice they destroy it. As Han Morgenthau has written,

> However much the content and objectives of today's ethics of nationalistic universalism may differ from those of primitive tribes or the

Thirty Years' War, they do not differ in the function which they fulfill for international politics, and in the moral climate which they create. The morality of the particular group, far from limiting the struggle for power on the international scene, gives that struggle a ferociousness and intensity not known to other ages. For the claim to universality which inspires the moral code of one particular group is incompatible with the identical claim of another group; the world has room for only one, and the other must yield or by destroyed. Thus, carrying their idols before them, the nationalistic masses of our time meet in the international arena, each group convinced that it executes the mandate of history, that it does for humanity what it seems to do for itself, and that it fulfills a sacred mission ordained by providence, however defined. Little do they know that they meet under an empty sky from which the gods have departed.[6]

For a nation, even more than for an individual, the truest morality is embodied in how it itself behaves rather than in how it tells or forces other to behave. Yet there is irony even here, for the nations that are restrained by their own moral principles may be hampered thereby in the struggle to survive; so that the application of moral principles to the conduct of policy may lead to the defeat or disappearance of those nations that are moral.

World Public Opinion

The application of moral principles to policy does not have the results that are intended in international affairs because it is a characteristic of international affairs that such principles cannot be applied uniformly. This is a problem that even some of the statesmen who have espoused idealism in foreign affairs have recognized. Woodrow Wilson and the other proponents of the League of Nations—the leaders whom E. H. Carr classified as idealists, and whom he attacked in *The Twenty Years' Crisis*—claimed to have solved the problem by calling on the

---

[6]Morgenthau, *Politics,* p. 263.

force of world public opinion. The independence of states could be restrained, they argued, and world public opinion had sufficient force to do it.

E. H. Carr quoted Lord Robert Cecil as a representative of this point of view. Lord Robert was perhaps the best-known British supporter of the League of Nations; and in explaining the provisions of the League Covenant to the House of Commons in 1919, he is quoted as having said that "What we rely upon is public opinion . . . and if we are wrong about it, then the whole thing is wrong." Explaining the League's functionings to the Imperial Conference of 1923, he said of the League that "its executive instrument is not force, but public opinion."[7]

As Carr saw it, the failure of public opinion to force the nations to preserve the peace meant the collapse of the idealistic theory of international relations that had been accepted in the 1920s. The premise of that theory had been that world public opinion was all that was necessary to do the job; and when the premise was shown to be false, the theory that had followed from it was invalidated. The failure of proponents of the idealistic theory to correctly forecast world events provided a dramatic illustration of this. Carr quoted Lord Robert Cecil as having told the Assembly of the League of Nations on September 10, 1931, that "there has scarcely ever been a period in the world's history when war seems less likely than it does at present."[8] Yet a mere eight days later the Japanese invaded Manchuria, and set off on the road that led to the Second World War.

Carr pointed out that public opinion was often weak, and also that it was often wrong.[9] For these reasons he believed that the idealists had been wrong to place their faith in it. There is, however, a more far-reaching explanation of why the premise that world public opinion would keep the peace was false. The truth of

---

[7]Carr, *Crisis*, p. 47.

[8]Carr, *Crisis*, p. 48.

[9]Carr, *Crisis*, pp. 50-51.

the matter is that world public opinion does not exist. Because nations are independent, the only public opinions that exist are national public opinions; and these display characteristics different from those with which Lord Robert Cecil and his colleagues endowed their hypothetical public opinion of the world.

In world affairs, appeals to public opinion are appeals to the public opinion of some other nation. If you and I, as American citizens, want to change the nature of the Soviet regime, it is of little use appealing to other Americans to agree with us. What we would have to do is somehow manage to communicate with the Russian people, manage somehow to persuade them that their government ought to be changed, and then figure out some way in which their desires in this respect could be carried into effect; all three of these are forbiddingly difficult to accomplish. The only way in which an appeal to our own American public opinion could be of any relevant force would be in attempting to persuade our own government to take or desist from certain actions with respect to the Soviet Union that we think might influence the behavior of the Soviet government, such as the legislation with respect to trade with the Soviet Union that may have led Russia to become less restrictive with respect to Jewish emigration.

Appealing to the public opinion of other countries, even when it can be done, is a tricky business. It is not only that, as E. H. Carr pointed out, public opinion is often wrong, but also that it is nationalistic and often resents advice or appeals from foreigners. It is difficult to persuade the population of another nation that its own expansionist policies, for example, should be resisted. As early as the fifth century B.C., when Thucydides described the politics of classical Greece, it was evident to close observers of political events that the public is easily carried away by enthusiasm for foreign conquests. Successes abroad are almost always popular. Expansionism is an attractive political program, so long as it does not cost too much. In modern times, there have been examples of tired populations being persuaded to abandon unsuccessful wars, as in turn the French and the Americans were in Indochina, and as the French were in Algeria; but it is less easy to think of nations that were persuaded to quit when they were winning or when their conquests were cheap and easy.

It also has become clear, as the twentieth century has gone on, that public opinion can be effectively and extensively manipulated by national governments. The invention of radio, of transistors, and of television has placed in the hands of governments a communications technology enabling them to control the minds of their subjects more completely than ever before. Contrary to what Lord Robert Cecil and the other proponents of the League of Nations predicted, the characteristic feature of the twentieth century has proved to be, not that public opinion tends to control governments, but that governments tend to control public opinion.

Moreover, national public opinion plays different roles in different nations. There are countries in which it is suppressed and plays no effective political role, and others in which it is of considerable importance. Many of the countries that most need to be restrained in their conduct do not, for practical purposes, have a public opinion at all. The force of public opinion is therefore of uneven application; and it is a typical irony of international relations that the regimes that it does inhibit are precisely those that one would least like to see weakened in the struggle for world survival.

Law

Some of the proponents of the League of Nations ideal thought that they had found another force in addition to that of public opinion upon which they could rely for support. It was the force of law. They would appeal to world law to enforce the rules of a new international order.

But law, like public opinion, is to be found within nations rather than above them. There is American law and Japanese law and Indian law, but there is no system of world law. E. H. Carr quite rightly wrote that it is confusing to speak of law in the abstract, as people do in such phrases as "the rule of law" which suggest that it is an abstract law that rules rather than (as is the case) human beings in its name. As Carr pointed out, any system of law (in the usual sense in which the word law is used) emanates from a political entity. There is no world state and therefore no world law.

Carr attacked the idealistic theory prevalent in the inter-war years according to which the establishment of a World Court would cause the world to be ruled by law. Human beings constituting a political entity would have to enforce those laws, as interpreted by the court; and, most important of all, the peoples of the world would have to accept and obey those laws, even if they were ordered not to do so by their national governments. But peoples in fact obey their own governments; and that was the crux of the issue that the framers of the League of Nations and the other idealists of the inter-war years refused to face. They could not (and did not even try to) change the political fact that states are independent; therefore the World Court could not rule the world, either by law or otherwise.

The proponents of the League of Nations ideal continued to be puzzled as to why this was so. They could see that the values they hoped to achieve in the world as a whole, such as peace and justice, were and are achieved within our respective countries by law. Law is used in this context as a kind of abstract shorthand word for a complex reality. A political society, acting through the various branches of its government, embodies and realizes its public moral values through commands of uniform application, called laws, which are interpreted and enforced through processes that are a part of the legal system. A law, or command, issued to the world as a whole would not have the same significance or effect, in the absence of the social and political context that *within* a country gives it its meaning: a unitary political society, a government, and the various processes through which governments

76

function. E. H. Carr correctly pointed out that it was not an abstraction called law that had brought peace and justice to the various countries, but rather the social and political realities in whose context law received its meaning.

In any event, what the statesmen and idealistic theorists of the 1920s had turned to was not law in the sense in which the term is used within countries, but rather law in the different, special, and somewhat misleading sense in which the *customs* of the European states in their dealings with one another, and their contractual promises to one another, once had been termed public international "law." Nations interpreted these traditions and treaties for themselves, except when they chose to let an international court or tribunal do it for them; and they also decided which international traditions of international conduct they would accept or reject, and which treaties they would recognize as being in force, or still valid, with respect to themselves. The specific prewar customs of the European states, which constituted the substantive contents of this supposedly paralegal system, were of no great value to the statesmen of the League, for they were the expression of the prewar international acceptance of war and its consequences, while what was sought in the 1920s was the abolition of war. What *was* thought to be of value was the confused pretense that customs and treaties constituted a kind of law that might be analogized to the legal systems within countries. In carrying out this pretense, the statesmen of the post-First World War era purported to create a new world order by entering into such treaties as the Covenant of the League of Nations and, in 1929, the Kellogg-Briand Pact to outlaw war as an instrument of national policy.

One of the confusions that this evidenced was the belief that a state entering into a contract is like a person doing so—which is not the case. One of the important differences is that a person is mortal, while a state may exist for a long time. Another difference is that a person, though he or she may change in some respects, will remain essentially the same throughout a lifetime. A state, however, changes its government, and over a longer period of time, changes its population. I am entitled to make commitments for myself, and therefore can sign a contract pledging that I will do something in ten years' time. But there is a real question as to whether today's president of the United States has a right to make a commitment on behalf of the person who will be president of the United States in ten years' time; and it is a real question whether today's Americans have a right to make a commitment that another generation of Americans will be expected to fulfill.

The third Marquess of Salisbury, the last of Queen Victoria's prime ministers, and perhaps the greatest of her foreign ministers, often used to make the point that it was undemocratic for an existing parliament to make a treaty commitment that would bind a future parliament: it was a practice, as he indicated, that would deny to the electorates of the future, and to their elected representatives, the right to make decisions for themselves.

Not merely is it, in the light of democratic principles, wrong; it is also futile. Governments refuse to be bound by past commitments that they find onerous; therefore such commitments cannot be relied upon. Historical experience has shown that the treaties most likely to be honored are those that are specific, relatively short-term, and not inconsistent with the perceived interests of the contracting states. This follows as a consequence of the independence of states, which allows states to decide for themselves whether or not to observe their treaty commitments.

In ancient times, it used to be thought that treaties were binding. The theory was that they were enforced by the gods before whom they were sworn. Mesopotamian treaties that date from the third millennium B.C. show the care that was taken to have oaths repeated in turn before each of the appropriate gods, and to provide the appropriate curses in each case for noncompliance.[10] The care that was taken attests to the reality of the belief. But the

---

[10]Donald L. Magnetti, "The Function of the Oath in the Ancient Near Eastern International Treaty," *American Journal of International Law*, Vol. 72 (October 1972), pp. 815, 816.

modern world does not share that faith. We do not believe that the gods enforce treaties and we are unable to point to any other entities that enforce them either.

The obvious difference between treaties and contracts is, indeed, that treaties are not enforceable; and it is this difference, even though it is not the only one, which was particularly noticed in the writings of the 1930s. It is clear that a state that violates a treaty commitment is not going to enforce the treaty against itself. It is clear, too, that no higher political authority, such as a world government, exists to enforce a treaty against a defaulting state. It is only the other states, then, that can act to enforce the treaty but what the writers of the 1930s had begun to see was that states would only act to enforce treaties if they deemed it to be in their own interest to do so.

E. H. Carr saw further. He saw that states acted in their own best interest when they did not have a treaty claim sanctioned by international law, and that they acted in precisely the same way when they did have such a treaty claim. He therefore observed that in the latter case they were not really enforcing international law, but were merely using international law as an ideological excuse for doing what they would have done in any event. Thus, the new international law was not a legal system at all; it was merely a disguise used by one set of contestants in the same old amoral, alegal, anarchic world of independent states.

Carr's book appeared before the final irony of the treaty system was revealed: that which concerned the Kellogg-Briand Pact. The Pact purported to outlaw aggressive war; an evident flaw in the reasoning behind it was that if a state violated the treaty by starting a war, the only way to enforce the treaty was for the other states to declare war upon the offender, so that a treaty, the purpose of which was to prevent warfare, in practice would call for the expansion of warfare.

An alternative approach to the problem posed by violation of the Kellogg-Briand Pact was the one developed at the Nuremberg trials after the second World War: that violations, while they could not be prevented, could at least be punished. That, of course, presupposes that every war will be won by the states that were the victims of aggression, which is not necessarily the case. The punishments inflicted by the tribunal at Nuremberg reflected a moral point of view, but not a legal one. It would only have been a legal process in the proper sense if, had the vanquished been able to institute charges and to prove their case in court, the Germans would have been entitled to have the American, British, and Russian victors punished.

The Nuremberg judgments should have been pronounced as an exception, not as a rule. In the unique circumstances created by the Nazi crimes against humanity, it was right only on this one occasion to disregard the conventions that would have protected the defendants against trial or punishment. But the judgments went further and purported not to be doing one-of-a-kind justice, but rather to be carrying into effect principles of general applicability; and as such, as a precedent in law, they were the undoing of centuries in which conscience had created civilization. For centuries, the European states had worked at, and had succeeded in, creating a code of conduct and courtesy in their dealings with one another that mitigated the harshness of the struggle for international power. It represented a triumph of civilization over savagery that they had learned to treat defeated foes with a measure of forebearance, and that as a matter of recognized right and established principle defeated adversaries and their leaders were allowed to keep their lives and liberties. If Nuremberg is considered not as an isolated episode, *sui generis,* but as a legal precedent, standing for the proposition that in future wars, too, the victors (who, for all we know, may be our adversaries) will execute the leaders of the vanquished, then, in the name of the futile Kellogg-Briand attempt to create a higher world order based upon law, international relations will have repealed the code of civilization and relapsed into barbarism.

Enforcement

As indicated before, the independence of states implies that in international relations there are no rules. In the 1930s, many of those who were thought of by themselves or by others as realists held the view that there were rules, but that the problem was that there was no enforcement of the rules. This was presented as a tough, no-nonsense way of thinking about international relations. What was needed, in this view, was the creation of an international police force; and that, supposedly, would put international politics on a par with domestic politics. Of course, it was a view that ignored the context in which police forces are able to function.

Police rarely have to use force. People tend to obey them, sometimes out of fear, sometimes out of loyalty to the state of which the police are the agency. Countries are not like people; countries are independent, and by definition do not do what others tell them to do unless forced to do so. When the police have to use force, they usually do not have to use very much. The typical lawbreaker has resources and powers that are minuscule in comparison to those of the state whose laws and authority he is challenging. In international affairs, it is otherwise: subduing a whole country tends to require a great deal of force. Armies, not police forces, must take the field in the uncertain hope of doing it.

Thus the creation of an international police force would be insufficient; an international army would be required, and it would have to be in perpetual war against the states of the world that assert their independent right to live according to their own rules—which is to say the international army would be matched against all of the world's independent states. Nor is it necessarily the case that those asserting and attempting to enforce rules of which you and I might approve would win these wars. Might would prevail. Within a society, might also prevails; but it is on society's side as against the individual criminal, so that the trial of

81

strength to which we refer as law enforcement will most times result in the triumph of what the society considers to be justice. In international affairs, on the contrary, the victory can go either way, and what is enforced might therefore turn out to be the opposite of a society's values, or its laws, or its notions of justice. The armies of all sides in an international conflict wear uniforms, and there is no objective way of determining which ones are the criminals and which ones are the police.

Indeed, these concepts, borrowed from domestic politics, are meaningless in world affairs. The attempt to apply them achieves results that are nonsensical. Within a country, the punishment or threat to punish whatever a government considers to be a crime generally achieves law and order; but in international affairs, it leads to lawless disorder, and continuous warfare of uncertain outcome and dubious value.

Sanctions

Some method of enforcement other than going to war had to be found if the theory that there are international rules was to be reconciled with the goal of achieving peaceful harmony among independent states. Sanctions were said to be the answer. Enforcement of justice by measures that fell short of war seemed to many in the League of Nations era to be a program that reconciled law with order. Non-recognition of those territorial gains that were achieved by aggression — though it was difficult to agree on a definition of aggression — was one such measure; economic embargoes were another. Since there was and is no higher world authority, each state, of course, would have to judge for itself what constitutes international wrongdoing; but the theory was that a consensus would emerge among the governments of the various states, and that they would then act together to impose sanctions against the state that they regarded as a transgressor. The sanctions would fall short of war, so that the peace of the world would not be disturbed, but the measures that were taken would exert real pressure, so that the program of enforcing international justice would have teeth in it. Such was the program. Its failure is well known. It did not deter Japan from occupying Manchuria, nor did it stop Mussolini from conquering Abbysinia. In the real world, self-interest restrains states from opposing acts of aggresssion, even on the rare occasions when there is general agreement that the acts complained of did in fact constitute aggression. Moreover, there is a strong economic incentive for private interests, too, to disregard embargoes; this was seen again in recent years in the long failure of economic sanctions to affect the policies of Mr. Ian Smith's white-supremacist Rhodesia.

Thus the sanctions by and large failed to materialize; but even if they had, the theory upon which they were based would have been invalidated. The theory was that if the sanctions proved effective, the state against which they were directed would concede the issue peacefully. But, as Stanley Baldwin said in 1934, "there is no such thing as a sanction which will work, which does not mean war."[11]

According to A. J. P. Taylor's account, and that of the military historian Sir Basil Liddell Hart and others, that is the explanation of how America was drawn into the Second World War; it was a story of an embargo that worked. The United States was persuaded that an embargo would force Japan to accept American terms peacefully. According to a recent history of Roosevelt's foreign policy, "only economic sanctions, Chiang Kai-shek told FDR, would force Japan into a negotiated settlement 'based on reason and justice.' Morgenthau, Ickes, Stanley K. Hornbeck, the State Department's senior Far Eastern adviser, Congressional leaders, and, according to an opinion poll, 75 percent of the American public agreed."[12] And all of them were wrong!

---

[11]Carr, *Crisis*, pp. 151–152.

[12]Robert Dallek, *Franklin D. Roosevelt and American Foreign Policy, 1932-1945* (New York: Oxford University Press, 1979), pp. 236–237.

In the summer of 1941, President Roosevelt brought sanctions to bear against Japan in consequence of Japanese expansion in the Far East, notably in Indochina; and the British and Dutch joined with the United States in the embargo. Three-quarters of Japan's foreign trade and nine-tenths of her oil supplies were cut off. It was the rare case of an embargo that proved to be effective. The Japanese military leadership, even though they may have been exaggerating the perils of the situation, calculated that the Japanese economy would collapse by the spring of 1942 unless the embargo were broken. They fixed November 25, 1941 as the date upon which it would become imperative for them to go to war if the embargo were not lifted. Efforts to negotiate the lifting of the embargo with the United States proved fruitless. On December 1, 1941, the Japanese Imperial Council decided that the national existence of Japan was at stake, and that it would be right to go to war in such a cause. On December 7, 1941, the Japanese attacked the American fleet at Pearl Harbor, and the two countries went to war.[13]

The theory that measures short of war could restrain international behavior failed to work when put into practice in the decade before the Second World War. Either the measures failed to be taken effectively, in which case they did not work; or else they were effective, in which case they led to war.

Peace and Justice

Enforcement, with or without war, is not the problem. The problem is that, because states are independent, in international relations there are no rules to enforce.

Within our societies we adopt rules that enable most of the world's countries to achieve peace and, according to some sort of

---

[13]A. J. P. Taylor, *The Second World War: An Illustrated History* (London: Hamish Hamilton, 1975), pp. 119–121. For Liddell Hart, see C. S. Ospina, "The War," *The Economist*, May 5, 1979, p. 8.

definition, justice. But when political leaders attempt in the spirit of such rules and in a straightforward way to achieve these same goals of peace and justice in world affairs, they obtain results that are unexpected. In the curious world of independent states, these goals, each difficult enough to achieve in its own right, are to a large extent antithetical.

Crusades on behalf of moral or legal principles represent a policy of war. Keeping the peace, on the other hand, means acquiescing in the many wrongs and injustices that are done in the world. Whereas within a society individuals subordinate themselves and tend not to put up a fight when society tries to stop them from doing what society considers to be wrong, states are independent, and have their own standards of right and wrong. A state that wants to impose its own notions of right and wrong on another state has to be prepared to go to war to do it.

In the twentieth century, those who concern themselves with these matters have been increasingly preoccupied with the dangers of modern warfare and the need for international peace. Perhaps the least unrealistic program for achieving it is embodied in the cartel-like concept of the United Nations Security Council. This was to be a bloc consisting of the governments of the nations that hold a preponderance of power in the world, not unlike the Concert of Europe in the nineteenth century. They were to seek an accommodation of views among themselves, presumably on a basis of mutual benefit, and then impose their decisions on the world. This was a conception that aimed at order, but it had nothing to do with justice; for it asserted the rights of the strong as against the weak, rather than of the weak as against the strong.

Domestic societies can live in peace and can at the same time achieve some sort of justice for their citizens. The independence of states means that countries, however, can work best for international peace by subordinating their notions of justice to the realities of power. Yet any political philosophy worthy of the name will tell us that a peace not based on justice cannot long endure. Is there a solution to the dilemma?

It is characteristic of international relations to lead to such dilemmas. When we try to achieve the moral and political values of our own country in the sphere of international relations, ironically, we achieve different and sometimes contrary results from those that we had intended. It is also ironic that if we do seem to attain one set of values that we cherish in international affairs, it has the unintended effect of destroying another set of values that we also cherish. As a final irony, the values we do seem to attain, at the expense of the others, are themselves ephemeral, and disappear when day is done.

If we are unprepared to go to war in a just cause, then we will be drawn into the war anyway, but at a less advantageous moment: that is the lesson of the 1930s. If we do go to war to achieve justice, we are troubled afterwards by the knowledge that war is itself unjust, and are haunted, as after Hiroshima and Nagasaki, by the demons that we have let loose in the world. If we choose to live in peace with an unjust status quo, we find that injustice brings political instability, and that the peace we purchased so dearly is illusory and explodes in revolutionary violence.

At the heart of the matter is the problem of change, which we regard as both inevitable and desirable, in the international sphere, where change is accomplished by warfare; and we confront this problem while believing a full-scale war might destroy the civilization that change is intended to advance.

6

THE BATTLEFIELDS
OF CHANGE

Mankind always has seen warfare as the most important thing
that happens in history. Those who broke the long silence
and had their messages carved in stone, the rulers of the ancient
world, chose above all to record in permanent form their battles,
their victories, and their conquests. Bards and thinkers were of the
same persuasion: epic was born from the war of Troy, and history
from the wars that the Greek city-states fought first against the
Persians and then against each other.

It may be objected that the genuinely important events in
history have been social or scientific, rather than political or
military; but mankind as a whole does not agree. It is typical that
in a recent issue of the New York *Times* (March 12, 1978) the
banner headline on the front page tells of perhaps twenty people
dying as a result of a raid by a small band of terrorists, while a
story given much lesser prominence, relegated to the bottom of
the page and continued on page 54, tells of astonishing claims by
scientists that they may be on the verge of discovering how the
universe began; how, and whether, it will end; and whether or
not there is a God. Presumably the order of priorities in allocating

front-page space reflects the experience of the editors as to what their readers consider to be most important.

It is in large part because the great issues of history are believed to depend upon the outcome of military campaigns that poets and novelists are haunted by the thought of lost battles that might have been won. Stendhal's Fabrice del Dongo, in the *Chartreuse de Parme*, represented the yearnings of a whole age in wanting to ride to victory with Bonaparte, and the frustration of the hopes of that age in arriving too late, in time only for Waterloo. The prevalent feeling of being born too late is closely associated with the notion that, had one been there, one might have turned the tides of battle. Archibald MacLeish took as his image the moment Charlemagne heard the summons to turn back, but too late, to save Roland, who was beleaguered in the mountain pass of Roncevaux; we too have heard the far-off sound, he wrote in the poem "The Too-Late Born." The tragedy of history is that one hears the horn of Roland too late; the premise of this view is that, had one arrived in time to enable Roland to win the battle, history could have had a happy ending.

The future too, and human hopes for it, traditionally have been seen in terms of battles and their outcome. Long ago it was prophesied to the Christian world that the ultimate triumph of good over evil would occur in a battle to be fought for control of the hill (in Hebrew, "har") at Megiddo ("Har Megiddo," or "Armageddon"), a strategic high point commanding the invasion route between Egypt and Mesopotamia.

In all of these cases, battles have seemed to be the events that change the world. That brings them into relation with politics, for the purpose of politics is to effect changes and to accommodate to change. But change is accomplished in different ways, depending upon whether the politics are international or domestic. In domestic politics, as we know them to be in mature societies today, government is the agency of change. Even those who had opposed the change tend to accept the government's decision because of an overriding loyalty to the political society itself or because they are coerced into doing so by the disparity in strength between society as a whole and individuals such as themselves. Thus, change is accomplished peacefully. In international affairs, war is the agency of change, and therefore is the functional equivalent of the domestic processes of government. Within a country, legislatures decree, judiciaries interpret, and executives enforce; but in the world of states, when irreconcilable conflicts arise, it is warfare that in effect does all three things, so that the major changes are accomplished by force.

Many of the great changes in political history are indeed due to war. Democracy, in terms of a wide extension of the franchise, began because the naval program that Themistocles devised for fifth-century Athens required mass manpower, and because the people, once they bore arms, could not be denied the right to participate in the political process. Many of the great advances in science and technology, opening up new possibilities for the human race, also emerged from the exertions of wartime. Atomic power is an obvious example, but of course there are many others. In modern times, however, there has been a great shift in sentiment, one result of which has been the general underestimation of the role played by warfare in promoting beneficial changes.

In the romantic imagination of the modern world, revolution brings change. The coming of the revolution is the millennium myth of the political left. War, on the contrary, has come to the thought of as a manifestation of reaction or right-wing politics. Thus in the eighteenth and nineteenth centuries, it was widely believed that wars were in the interests of princes but not of peoples, and that the overthrow of monarchical government and its replacement by republican government would bring perpetual peace.[1] Similarly, in the twentieth century, Marxists have argued that warfare is a manifestation of imperialism, and will come to an end when, in its dying phase, capitalism meets its fated doom.

Yet when one thinks back to the objectives of left-wing

---

[1]Kenneth N. Waltz, *Man, the State and War: A Theoretical Analysis* (New York: Columbia University Press, 1959), p. 101.

thought of about a century or two ago, it is curious to note that it is warfare, rather than revolution, that has brought about the principal changes that progressive opinion then desired. Two of three multinational empires that oppressed the peoples of Europe and Asia were overthrown in the First World War; and there was even a moment that the third, the Russian empire, as well as the Habsburg and Ottoman empires, seemed on the verge of dissolution. Earlier, the aspirations of the German and Italian peoples to achieve national unity were achieved through warfare. In Russia, the overthrow of the czar and his eventual replacement by Lenin were in large part a consequence of the war against Germany. In more recent times, the destruction of colonial empires, and the emergence of independent nations in Africa, Asia, and the Middle East were the result, directly or indirectly, of the Second World War and of the colonial wars that were its aftermath.

On the other hand, the changes wrought by revolution are less evident. From a certain point of view, one could argue, for example, that the Russian revolutions, to the extent that they were not externally caused, were devoid of significant effect. A dictator (emperor) was overthrown, but he was replaced by another. The czarist secret police forces were replaced by the Bolshevik secret police forces. Economic development moved along at about the same pace that might have been projected had the czar remained in power. Disproportionately large armed forces are still maintained. There is still censorship. Artistic policy is still reactionary. An empire is still maintained over the Turkic and other peoples of middle Asia. Anti-Semitism continues to flourish. Expansionist foreign policy objectives remain the same. There is the same geopolitical drive to the south, bringing pressure on Turkey and Iran; the goal of dominating Afghanistan that remains the same; the pressure eastward, as before, directed against China and Japan; the hegemony over Poland and eastern Europe that was so important, too, to the czars.

Thus it can be argued that nothing fundamental was changed, and that the revolutionary uprisings of 1917 had political consequences that were essentially conservative. Revolutions, in the end, leave things as they are. War, not revolution, is the principal agency of change in the political world, even of left-wing change. The internal tendencies and dispositions of a nation seem to be so persistent that even revolutions do not often leave lasting effects; whereas war, wrought by mutually alien forces, leads to terrible and marvelous changes that are often of fundamental significance.

The invasion of a neighboring state may be a deplorable act, but it is hard to think of any other way in which such welcome events as the overthrow of the Pol Pot regime in Cambodia or the Idi Amin regime in Uganda could have been brought about. As a recent article in *The Economist* well put it,

> In a better world, there might be effective means—ideally, non-military ones—for the international community to make a tyrannical regime mend its way, or end its sway. In today's world there are not. Even the economic sanctions provided for in the U.N. charter, which have never yet been wholeheartedly applied, and cannot be so applied if the offender is protected by a veto-wielding power, are applicable only when a threat to international peace has been identified.
>
> However fearsome a sovereign government's treatment of its subjects, however loud the chorus of international indignation, there are only two accepted ways of bringing it down. Either its own people succeed in freeing themselves (and the more ruthless it is, the less their chances of doing so); or an external conflict makes an end of it—as happened in Cambodia and Uganda this year, and for that matter in Germany in 1945.[2]

In a world of independent states, war is inevitable because change is inevitable, and war is the only process in international affairs for effecting contested changes. To the extent that change is desirable, war is also, therefore, desirable—or so it once seemed to be; but now it no longer does, and that is a central problem—some would say *the* central problem—of the modern world.

---

[2]"Installed by Invasion," *The Economist*, April 21, 1979, p. 16.

From earliest times there have been individual artists, philosophers, and prophets who saw war as evil. Euripides took as one of his subjects the most glorious triumph that his nation had ever won, and pictured its real consequences: "A solitary old woman with a dead child in her arms; that, on the human side, is the result of these deeds of glory."[3] Hebrew prophets, taking a similar view of warfare, foresaw the coming of a better world, in which the nations would renounce war and beat swords into plowshares.

But these have been isolated voices and visions, and for the most part, war has been accepted as a normal part of international life. That seems to be no longer the case, insofar as opinion in the advanced industrialized states of the Northern Hemisphere is concerned. Perhaps it is because the expectations that are aroused in modern societies, insulated from many of life's hazards, lead us to the belief that life can be lived in safety and security. Certainly it is, in part, because of the terrible destruction that weapons now can cause, making it seem that another world war would be so dreadful that it cannot happen. Perhaps it is for other reasons as well; but somewhere along the way, modern society began to believe that wars belong to the savage past and no longer should be expected to occur.

One evening, about 40 years ago, in the rain forests of South America near the headwaters of the Amazon, an American explorer was talking to a clan chieftain of the Jivaro headhunters about the causes of blood feuds. The American felt admiration and affection for the Jivaro, and had travelled across the Andes mountains to their jungle to live with them and to study them. One of the things about them that interested him, he used to say, was why a man would cut off another man's head, shrink it to the size of his fist, and then dance around it; and he hoped that the Jivaro would explain their peculiar custom to him.

---

[3]Gilbert Murray, *Euripides and His Age,* 2nd Ed. (London, New York, and Toronto: Oxford University Press, Geoffrey Cumberlege, 1946), p. 87.

The chieftain, Chumbika, was planning to take revenge for the death of his brother. A tree had fallen on the brother and killed him. Chumbika believed that a magical curse had caused this to happen. A witch-doctor had been consulted, and had divined the name of a member of an enemy tribe as the author of the curse. Chumbika proposed to kill the man and take his head.

The American pointed out that sometimes trees fall because they have died or because they have been undermined by flood water. He suggested that the tree might have fallen by accident. "Death is never an accident," Chumbika said. "Nothing is an accident. Everything that happens has a cause, a death above all, because death is not natural. Life is natural. Life is what we all have, what everything has. When life is taken away, someone must take it. . . ." He went on to say that white people "no longer understand these things. You do not see the truth that life is natural and death caused only by the power of an enemy's demon."[4]

The Jivaro Indians had not been puzzled by the observation that, over the course of many generations, everybody dies, and nobody above a certain age remains alive. Or perhaps they had not made the observation. Whenever a relative died, the Jivaro were surprised and angry; and they went to the witch-doctor to ask whom to blame and punish.

When the explorer bade farewell to his Indian friends, he left the jungles of Latin America and returned to the United States. There his countrymen believed, as they still believe, that normally their country is at peace with the rest of the world. Yet the country won its independence in one war against Great Britain and not long afterwards fought another one. Wars against the American Indians were waged regularly from colonial days until the 1890s. Wars were waged against Mexico with some frequency. Some expected the wars to end when the United States reached its

---

[4]Lewis Cotlow, *Amazon Head-Hunters* (London: Robert Hale Limited, 1954), p. 49

present continental frontiers, but in 1898 America declared war against Spain and seized territories not merely in the Caribbean but also on the far side of the Pacific. The United States, not long before the explorer's return, had been drawn into what was then called the Great War and is now called the First World War. Many historians and public men had tried to identify the culprits who had caused the war to occur. In the United States Senate, an investigation focused on the allegation that certain armaments manufacturers, such as the sinister Basil Zaharoff, had caused the war, and should be curbed or punished. Progressive opinion held that another war would never occur. Later, when Germany, Italy, and Japan noticeably began to threaten the peace, it was right-wing opinion that held that war need not occur, unless Jews or other unpopular groups were permitted to cause it to occur.

The Second World War became yet another war to end all wars, but afterwards America felt obliged to enter two major wars in Asia and several minor wars elsewhere. This was only the tip of the iceberg; war was contemplated and risked many times more. A recent study by the Brookings Institution has shown that between 1946 and 1975, the United States threatened to use military force in order to achieve its objectives on 215 separate occasions, or, on an average of once every other month.[5] Nonetheless Americans continued to regard the outbreak of war as a surprising event that ought never to occur, and that required explanation and punishment of the guilty parties, if ever it should happen to occur.

The explorer of Latin American jungles meanwhile, in books, lectures, and films has continued to retell the story of Chumbika the headhunter. His audiences in the United States continue to marvel at the mental childishness of the Indians who did not see that, since people die all the time, death is something that is to be expected in the normal course of events.

---

[5] Cited in Alan Wolfe, "The Cycles of Belligerency," *The Nation,* February 3, 1979, p. 104.

Progressive opinion in most of the civilized world now sees war as abnormal and preventible, but has not come to grips with the problem of international change. American and European idealists whose program calls essentially for a permanent world-wide cease-fire agreement fail to understand that those who are dissatisfied with the location of the cease-fire line regard such a program as a hypocritical excuse for keeping ill-gotten gains. At a small meeting more than a decade ago, I heard an American lady of militantly leftist views say to a visiting friend of Mao Tse Tung's: "When you go back to China, tell Chairman Mao that the American *people* want peace!" She was surprised to be told that Mao would not understand her message in the sense that she intended it. Mao, according to his friend, wanted to change the world; and basic changes could be made only by fighting for them. Mao recognized that the vested interests defending the status quo would use peace slogans as part of their propaganda—such slogans as the American lady had used—even though in fact the imperialists (as he considered them to be) would not give up their unjust privileged positions without a fight. Of course, they wanted peace in the sense of being left in undisturbed possession of their vested interests. Mao believed above all in change, and did not see the possibility of radical change being brought about by peaceful means. He was a prophet: he brought not peace, but a sword.

In those days—the middle of the 1960s—it was widely believed in the United States that the Chinese leadership did not understand that the invention of nuclear and other modern weapons had transformed the circumstances in which the battles of world politics now will be fought. Carl von Clausewitz had taught that wars have to be fought in such a way as to conform to political objectives; but weapons that might destroy the whole world would thereby defeat the political objective in the service of which they were used. Any war between minor countries, in a world of superpowers with global interests, could involve and eventually bring in major countries; and since any war between the major countries seemed likely to involve nuclear weapons, or other weapons of mass destruction, it followed that war has become irrational and obsolete.

This is a conclusion that Americans had drawn from the events that ended the Second World War, and they were surprised that the Chinese leadership was reported to have not drawn these same conclusions. To Americans it seemed clear, in the aftermath of Hiroshima and Nagasaki, that wars have become so dangerous that, in the future, they would not and should not be allowed to occur. It was not clear who was going to prevent them, nor was it clear how international conflicts were going to be resolved without them; yet there was a feeling that something, somehow, would be done, because warfare, which had always been homicidal, now had become suicidal as well.

To the extent that this represented a prophecy that there would be no more wars after 1945, it could hardly have been more wrong. All of the great powers have been involved since then in wars or invasions, except for Germany and Japan, who were defeated in the Second World War and have not fully rearmed. The permanent members of the Security Council of the United Nations—the Soviet Union, the United States, China, Britain, and France—all have invaded other countries during this period. There have been wars or invasions involving Greece, Turkey, Cyprus, Malaysia, Nigeria, Tanzania, India, Pakistan, Bangladesh, Uganda, Rhodesia, South Africa, Algeria, Zaire, Cuba, Egypt, Israel, Jordan, Syria, Hungary, Czechoslovakia, Ethiopia, Somalia, Holland, Indonesia, Laos, Cambodia, Vietnam, Morocco, Mauritania, Portugal, Angola, Iran, Iraq, Afghanistan, Ecuador, Peru, Libya, Chad, both Koreas, both Yemens—and others as well.

The world since 1945 has been at war almost continuously, even though the citizens of the prosperous countries have been sufficiently unaffected to be able to pretend that they have been living in a world at peace. Warfare has been adapted to the requirements of today's world. The states of the world have accommodated to the new dangers posed by weapons of mass destruction by fighting wars of limited scope. Hiroshima caused subsequent wars to be restrained rather than abolished. In its restrained form, warfare has continued to rule the world. The great issues still are settled on the battlefield.

Yet the danger persists. Despite the overriding importance of doing so, we have not been able to devise a program that effectively guarantees that weapons of mass destruction never will be used. It is a goal that continues to elude us. As a consequence, there is always the terrible chance that the next war might be the one that bursts out of control and brings the world to an end. Therefore, it remains true that the problem of our time is the necessity of abolishing warfare, in the context of an international political structure that makes warfare inevitable.

Within domestic political structures, warfare between the opponents and proponents of political change is not normal. An overriding loyalty to a political entity higher than their own faction can and generally does lead all sides to subordinate their differences to a common allegiance. In order to make this happen in today's world, it seems obvious, as Hans Morgenthau and others have pointed out, that we will have to create a world state and a world government, and that the primary political loyalty of all mankind must be to the world as a whole. The difficulties and dangers of accomplishing these ends are obvious.

Thus the dilemma of the need for war, caused by the need for change, in a world which also needs peace more than ever because of the destructive magnitude of today's weapons, has to be considered in the light of the age-old dream that there might be something larger than the state, and that the state might therefore be, or might become, subordinate rather than independent, and therefore defer to the requirements of a larger entity.

7

WIDER LOYALTIES

From earliest times, political civilization has consisted of a multiplicity of independent states. The world of the third millenium B.C. as portrayed in the inscriptions unearthed at Ebla,[1] is in this respect the same as the world of today.[2] Yet the myths, prevalent in so many times and places, that tell of the common origin of various peoples, or of the common origin of mankind as a whole, suggest a similarly ancient and widespread awareness that political loyalties might extend beyond the frontiers of one's own particular state — that there could or should be a higher loyalty. The historical literature of classical Greece, which is the earliest such literature that has come down to us, shows that this possibility already had passed into the forefront of consciousness; Herodotus was inspired by it, as was Aeschylus in *The*

---

[1]The thousands of clay tablets recovered from the ancient royal archives of Ebla, in northern Syria, contain accounts of international wars, treaties, and trade in a context that suggests Syria at the time was a patchwork of independent city-states, engaged in the usual rivalries.

[2]Chaim Bermant and Michael Weitzman, *Ebla: A Revelation in Archaeology* (New York: Times Books, 1979).

Persians, while Thucydides was haunted by its subsequent failure.

The events narrated by Herodotus and Thucydides continue to be discussed with passionate interest because they raise timeless questions. In fact, they happened long ago, but in essence they are happening all the time. Twenty-five hundred years ago, Athens, Sparta, and a number of other Greek states joined together to defeat the Persian empire; but once the Greeks had beaten the common enemy, their unity fell apart, and they turned on one another. In the liberating wars against Persia, the citizens of the independent Greek city-states had learned to think of themselves as members of an overall Hellenic community. But when their unity of purpose collapsed, and the fear of Persia no longer drew them together, the Greeks seemed to look only to the individual self-interest of their own city-states, and they fought against one another at least as fiercely as previously they had fought against the foreigners. Had the community of Hellas then been a mere illusion? Or was it real, and were those who now fought the inter-Greek wars morally and politically blind to its reality?

Similar questions have been debated often. The sixteenth-century Spanish theologians who wrote about what we now call international law thought in terms of the community of Christendom; and in the eighteenth century, Voltaire and Gibbon wrote about the republic of Europe as though it were a single commonwealth. Others, on the contrary, saw the individual states, such as England and France, as the highest political reality, and thought either that these states would or that they should pursue no more than their own particular interests.

Loyalty to the state pulls one way; loyalty to a larger entity pulls another way. The tension between the two is one of the constants of political discourse and, when the claims of the two become incompatible, one of the tragedies of political drama.

The Community of Culture

In 1979 and 1980, press reports seemed to pose the question of whether the Khomeini revolution in Iran meant that militant Islam was reviving and would unite against the West. After the American and European public began to be aware of the depth of the split between Shia and Sunni Moslems, the question became whether the mullahs of Iran would be able to ignite a Shia uprising that would erase ethnic and state frontiers.

When the Sunni government of an Iraq that is more Shia then Sunni ordered an invasion of Shia Iran in 1980, the question was answered. National loyalties overcame religious ones. Certainly, the contrary pull of competing loyalties caused strain, and the Iraqi government eventually may pay a penalty for causing that strain: Shia Iraq someday may rise up against its Sunni government. But that would be a matter of internal politics. Insofar as international politics are concerned, the immediate verdict was that of *The Economist:* "The ethnic bond has survived the Iran-Iraq war in better shape than the religious one: against a lot of people's expectations, Iranians remained loyal to Iran and Iraqis to Iraq, regardless of whether they were Shia Moslems or Sunni Moslems."[3] The pull of religious culture, or indeed of any culture, may be strong; but the pull of nationalism is greater.

The wars between the Greek city-states of the fifth century B.C., too, took place within the framework of a common culture. So did the wars between the city-states of Sumer, in southern Mesopotamia, five thousand years ago. So did the medieval wars within Christendom and within Islam. In all these cases, it was a culture that was the entity larger than the state. Cultures rest on such bases as a shared religious outlook and on common values. Language can have a unifying effect too; Latin was the language of literate Christendom, and French was the common language of

---

[3]*The Economist,* December 13, 1980, special section, "The Gulf: a survey," p. 22.

European diplomacy. An easy flow of persons and transactions between the states goes into the making of a culture, as does intermarriage among the leadership groups, also as does the formation of business, professional, guild, or fraternal organizations that cross the lines of frontiers, bringing an interconnection and in some respects an interdependence of economic systems.

In one crucial respect, however, a culture falls short of forming a political society. "Society" derives from a Latin word that meant "an associate"; and a society is a group of persons who have associated together in furtherance of some common purpose or enterprise. The tragedy of cultures such as those of Sumeria, classical Greece, and Europe before the First World War, was that they were not able to achieve a political society; the populations of their constituent states did not come together to work towards a common political purpose.

Certain common political tendencies can be observed, however, in the inter-state behavior that takes place within cultural frameworks. Moral approval tends to attach to a somewhat even distribution of power between the states, so that an attempt by one state at aggrandizement is viewed by the others not merely as frightening but also as wrong. Intricate balances of power develop both in practice and in theory, as they did in Greece before Alexander, and among the city-states of the Italian renaissance. Continuous intercourse breeds quarrels, so that warfare tends to be endemic, but also limited in scope and in purpose, as in Sumeria of the third millenium B.C. and in the Europe of the *ancien regime*.[4] A discrimination tends to be made between those states that fall within the cultural framework, which are treated in accordance with certain standards of decency, courtesy, and fair play, and states outside the ambit of the

---

[4]Endemic among the Sumerian states: William H. McNeill, *The Rise of the West: A History of the Human Community* (Chicago and London: University of Chicago Press, 1963), p. 43. Limited goals of the Sumerian wars: Chester G. Starr, *A History of the Ancient World* (New York: Oxford University Press, 1965), p. 45.

culture, which can be treated unscrupulously, as the Spanish con-
quistadors treated the Indian empires of the New World. This
discrimination tends to be embodied in a more or less elaborate
body of inter-state customs that are applicable only to relations
between the states that are within the culture, and which come to
be regarded as a code of international law.

If the culture as a whole is physically secure from outside attack, the mitigation of the harshness of inter-state relations within
the culture tends to obscure the importance of frontiers and the
reality of power rivalries. A false sense of security is induced. A
sense develops that mankind has advanced and matured, and
that the bad old days of history have been left behind. John
Maynard Keynes described that sense at the beginning of *The
Economic Consequences of the Peace,* when he wrote his famous
description of what life was like in Great Britain just before the
First World War:

> The inhabitant of London could order by telephone, sipping his morn-
> ing tea in bed, the various products of the whole earth, in such quan-
> tity as he might see fit, and reasonably expect their early delivery upon
> his doorstep; he could at the same moment and by the same means
> adventure his wealth in the natural resources and new enterprises of
> any quarter of the world, and share, without exertion or even trouble,
> in their prospective fruits and advantages; or he could decide to cou-
> ple the security of his fortunes with the good faith of the townspeople
> of any substantial municipality in any continent that fancy or infor-
> mation might recommend. He could secure forthwith, if he wished it,
> cheap and comfortable means of transit to any country or climate
> without passport or other formality, could despatch his servant to the
> neighboring office of a bank for such supply of the precious metals as
> might seem convenient, and could then proceed abroad to foreign
> quarters, without knowledge of their religion, language, or customs,
> bearing coined wealth upon his person, and would consider himself
> greatly aggrieved and much surprised at the least interference. But,
> most important of all, he regarded this state of affairs as normal, cer-
> tain, and permanent, except in the direction of further improvement,
> and any deviation from it as aberrant, scandalous, and avoidable. The
> projects and politics of militarism and imperialism, of racial and

cultural rivalries, of monopolies, restrictions, and exclusion, which were to play the serpent to this paradise, were little more than the amusements of his daily newspaper, and appeared to exercise almost no influence at all on the ordinary course of social and economic life, the internationalization of which was nearly complete in practice.[5]

The awakening from that sort of dream can be terrible. There is a feeling that all basic assumptions and beliefs have been invalidated, and that nothing is left that it is safe to hold onto. The search for what is profoundly real begins anew. It was in such circumstances—those of a world that seemed to be shattered—that Thucydides questioned the meaning of history, and that Plato examined the purpose of politics; and in such circumstances, too, political philosophers since the end of the First World War have tried to understand the nature of politics among nations.

The emotional starting point for the inquiry is something that is true only in a subjective sense: it is the feeling that the tragedy that happened was a civil war. Sir Leonard Woolley, the excavator of Ur, caught that feeling when he portrayed the inter-state wars of Sumeria 5,000 years ago as a kind of civil war.[6] From the classical Athenian dramatists as well as from Thucydides, one gets the sense that the wars between the Greek city-states were the civil wars of an Hellenic civilization. The events of the First World War, and the conflicts that divided Europe from 1919 until the American entry into the Second World War in 1941, were felt by participants (and are seen by historians) to be a European civil war.[7]

The opposition between the subjective truth that it was civil war and the objective truth that it was international war mirrors

[5]John Maynard Keynes, *The Economic Consequences of the Peace* (New York: Harcourt, Brace and Howe, 1920), pp. 11–12.

[6]C. Leonard Woolley, *The Sumerians* (New York: W.W. Norton & Company, Inc., The Norton Library, 1965), pp. 62–89.

[7]D. C. Watt, "European Military Leadership and the Breakdown of Europe, 1919-1939," in Adrian Preston, ed., *General Staffs and Diplomacy Before The Second World War* (London: Croom Helm; Totowa, New Jersey: Rowman and Littlefield, 1978), pp. 9–22.

the opposition between loyalty to a whole culture and loyalty to a particular state. When conflicts occur — and they are bound to occur as long as there is more than one state — it is the political loyalty to the state that takes precedence, even though the resulting battles seem fratricidal. Yet both loyalties are real, and that is the heightened tragedy of such conflicts; the mark of Cain is upon them.

The loyalties can be reconciled, and the tension ended, only by constructing a single political society, expressing itself through a united state, on the basis of a common culture. This is what the late Jean Monnet aimed at (with what amount of success, we still do not know) in attempting to forge today's multiple sovereignties into a Common Market that would become one Europe. It is what the Arabic peoples have failed to do, despite a common language, religion, and ethnic background, and despite the professed desire of many of their leaders. It is what George Washington, James Madison, Alexander Hamilton, John Jay, and their colleagues succeeded in doing when they joined thirteen different English-speaking states into the United States of America. The record of many failures and few successes shows how difficult a thing it is to accomplish.

The Community of Belief

Ideological movements, too, can be seen as entities larger than the world's individual states. Especially in the twentieth century, it has been thought that the broad appeal of secular ideologies might overshadow popular allegiance to particular countries. It is one of the things that John Maynard Keynes meant when, on returning from Russia in 1925, he wrote that Bolshevism was a religion and that Lenin was "a Mahomet, not a Bismarck."[8]

---

[8]John Maynard Keynes, *Essays in Persuasion* (New York: Harcourt, Brace & Company, 1932), pp. 297, 299.

A reading of history should have shown that governments tend to use ideologies, rather than the other way round. Constantine became Christian and therefore made his empire become Christian. Mohammed and his successors carved out an empire that was obliged to accept Mohammedanism. At the end of the Second World War, the Red Army occupied eastern Europe and forced it to become communist. Governments push their ideologies onto their subjects. But somehow the opposite is thought to be true: that governments are ruled by ideologies. Certainly, it is true that sometimes governments act from ideological motives. But much more often they do not; and to the extent that they involve themselves at all in these matters, it is to use the very real propaganda power of ideology to mobilize mass support for policies that have worldly and quite non-ideological objectives.

Americans, in particular, have been prone to be taken in by a belief that ideology governs political behavior. In the circumstances, it is natural; the mass immigration of diverse peoples into the United States in the course of our existence has made it plausible to think of America itself as an idea rather than a nation. While the population of France is overwhelmingly of French origin going back many centuries, and the population of Italy is Italian, and of Germany, German in the same sense, Americans come from countries all over the world and are made one only by their common allegiance. It is normal that Americans should seek to apply their own experience to others, and to imagine that others, too, should allow their commitment to political beliefs and constitutional ideals to override clannish ethnic loyalties. Yet the American experience is unique, and the attempt to apply it elsewhere has resulted in a basic and continuing misunderstanding of world events.

The hopes and the fears of American administrations throughout this century in large part have been inspired by ideological appeals. The hopes have been inspired by the ideology of peaceful cooperation between states, within the treaty

106

framework of the Kellogg-Briand pact to outlaw aggressive war, or within the institutional framework of the League of Nations, the United Nations, the two World Courts, various arbitral tribunals, regional organizations, and international functional bodies and agencies. The dashing of these hopes in the many and bloody wars of the twentieth century is the subject of much of the literature of international relations.

But the mistaken fears have caused even more damage than have the misplaced hopes. In our time, the ideology that the United States has feared the most is world communism. Perhaps the answer to the most important analytical question that American foreign policy has confronted since 1945 has been affected by this fear: the question of the balance of priorities between the requirements of communist ideology and those of traditionally imperialistic Russian state interests in the decision-making process in the Soviet Union. It becomes an even more complicated question to answer if one allows for the possibility that the Soviet leaders delude themselves as well as others, and that they talk themselves into believing that they are advancing the utopian goals of communism when in fact they are merely acting as dictators and traditional Russian imperialists like the czars.

In analyzing and predicting Soviet behavior, the answer to this question always has made a difference. In analyzing the role of the international communist movement, for a time it did not. Believing that the communist parties throughout the world, when in opposition, or when kept in power by Russian bayonets, accept direction and money from the Soviet Union, successive American administrations in the 1940s and 1950s considered the world communist movement to be a monolithic conspiracy directed from Moscow; and that was a position that was quite right from either the point of view of those who think in terms of ideology or those who think in terms of national interest.

However, when communist parties seized power in various countries on their own (as distinct from being installed in power by the Russian army), the situation changed. The leaders of

107

states, whether communist or not, are driven to assert the ambitions and interests of their states; nationalism, history, and geography generally prove to be deeper and more compelling factors than are creeds and theories. Moreover, political leaders, once they rise to the top, are tempted to assert their own theories, their own interpretations, and their own policies. To the extent that circumstances free them to do so, communist leaders, like any other leaders, seem to want to carry out their own programs. This brings them to the first imperative of international relations: a country must be independent in order to carry its own programs into effect, and to be independent, a country must have enough power to fight off the attempts by other countries to control it. Thus the internal logic of international relations tends toward the dissolution of the world communist movement that the Russians had created for the purpose of furthering their own hegemonial ambitions.

Communism now has rival national centers. As time goes on, it seems likely that more such centers will develop. For the United States it is important to recognize that the rival governments do claim to regard themselves as communists, and therefore profess a faith which is hostile to our own and to which we in turn are therefore hostile. They will be less dangerous to us, however, if we make use of the knowledge that they also have become hostile to one another.

The failure of successive American administrations to see what had happened seems to have come from a failure to understand the full consequences of the fact that the world is composed of states that are independent. Wilsonian hopefulness, and the fearfulness of monolithic communism, both are aspects of the same error, which overestimates the force of global ideology because it underestimates the force of states, and particularly of national states, in the exercise of their independence. The price that the United States has had to pay for this error, and that the peoples of the world have been made to pay, is appallingly high. This is particularly clear if one looks at the record of American policy in Asia.

The nature of that policy continues, of course, to be the subject of disagreement; so it may be useful if I outline the broad lines of what I believe that policy to have been. It was not, in my view, a policy of support for democratic regimes in that part of the world. If it had been, then, no matter whether we won or lost, we could have been proud of ourselves. We cannot expect other states to behave in accordance with their proclaimed beliefs, but there are times when we do so ourselves; and however unwise that may be, at least we have the satisfaction of knowing that we have behaved in a principled way. But that was not the case in respect of the political and military battle waged by the United States for a quarter of a century against Asian communism.

No democratic alternative was available in countries such as China, Korea, and Vietnam. I cannot believe that high officials of the American government ever considered the regimes that we supported in those countries to be genuine democracies. What we opposed was the alternative to them—the hostile force that we thought emanated from the Soviet Union. This was not a revolutionary foreign policy program on our part, aiming at the triumph of our ideals throughout the world; it was a traditional foreign policy program, aiming to stop the threatened advance of a hostile force. It is within the power politics terms of this traditional sort of foreign policy objective that I judge the American strategy in Asia to have been misconceived. The sort of thing that successive American governments did not see was that, in order to meet the Soviet threat, what was important was that the power of China should be organized, and what was relatively unimportant was which persons or parties did the organizing

In the late 1940s and 1950s, the chief foreign policy concern of the United States was the containment of Soviet expansion. Germany was divided, and Japan was disarmed; China was the only potentially great Power left on the frontiers of the Soviet empire that might provide a counter-balance to the Russian drive to expand. Because of the independence of states, any great Powers that border one another are in a situation that fosters conflict; and in fact China and Russia have a history of rivalry and conflict. It was predictable — and indeed it was predicted by keen students of nationalism such as General Charles de Gaulle — that China and Russia would quarrel,[9] and if Russian expansion was what the United States wanted to deter, then the aid and encouragement of the development of China's power was the logical policy to pursue. Perversely, the United States did just the reverse. China was opposed at every step. The Korean war was waged in such a way that China was provoked to enter it against the UN forces; and the United States did everything that might have been calculated to force China back into the Soviet camp.

As the American government saw it, the Chinese leadership did not constitute an independent entity. Mao, Chou, and their colleagues in the government at what we still called Peiping were not Chinese; they were merely Russians wearing masks. On May 18, 1951, Dean Rusk, then Assistant Secretary of State for Far Eastern Affairs and later Secretary of State, told his audience at the China Institute that "We do not recognize the authorities in Peiping for what they pretend to be. The Peiping regime may be a colonial Russian government. . . . It is not the Government of China. It does not pass the first test. It is not Chinese."[10]

To the extent that the U.S. genuinely was pursuing as its geopolitical goal the containment of Russian expansion in Asia, it was mistaken in opposing China and therefore was fortunate that its opposition to China proved ineffective. Chinese unity and power grew despite American opposition. In 1978, the Carter administration made explicit its view that China could help to block Soviet expansion. If the Carter administration was correct in this assessment — which I think exaggerates current, as distinct from potential, Chinese power — it is no thanks to our own policy that

---

[9]This does not mean that they must always quarrel; it means only that this situation tends to foster conflict.

[10]Quoted in Roger Hilsman, *To Move a Nation: The Politics of Foreign Policy in the Administration of John F. Kennedy* (Garden City, New York: Doubleday & Company, Inc., 1967), p. 295.

we have available to us this important resource. We fought to prevent it from coming into being.

In the 1960s, it was Chinese expansion in its own right that had become the chief fear of the Kennedy and Johnson administrations—China as China, instead of China as Russia. The Russians, it was thought, were maturing and becoming members of the club; it was the Chinese who were the world's outlaws. It was thought obvious that the Chinese would drive south, and it was thought that stopping them from doing so might be as important as once it was to stop German expansion in Europe.

In January of 1965, a senior State Department official gave me some indication of the official thinking along these lines when I asked him to pass along some suggestions to his colleagues. I made the point that if our concern—our genuine concern— was to prevent Chinese expansion southwards, the obvious policy to pursue was to support the strongest national leader who stood in their path. As everybody agreed that this was Ho Chi Minh of northern Vietnam, Ho and his movement seemed to be the ones we ought to consider supporting, no matter how much we might disapprove of their domestic politics. My friend in the State Department declined to pass along the suggestion, even for the purpose of stimulating discussion among his colleagues; he said that the only question that it would raise in their minds was the question of my patriotism.

The United States in 1965 entered into a full-scale war against Vietnam with the curious stated objective of stopping the Chinese, who were Vietnam's historic enemies. The leaders of the American government at that time seemed to see no difference between the Vietnamese and the Chinese; they seemed to view all communists as the same.

After a while, it became the Vietnamese who were the chief enemy, though that meant that there was no rational purpose the war was meant to serve, since Vietnam did not threaten the territory or interests of the United States, and Indochina was of no intrinsic importance to American world policy. Feeling impelled to enlarge American participation in the war into Laos and Cam-

111

bodia, the United States contradicted the assumptions upon which it had gone to war when it turned to Russia, and, during the Nixon administration, to China, to ask their help in getting the Indochinese to accept a compromise peace; for if Russia and China were on such good terms with us, against whose communist empire had we been waging the costly and bloody war? What a long road the United States had travelled! We fought the Chinese on the theory that they were agents of Soviet Russia, and we had fought the Vietnamese on the theory that they were agents of the Chinese, who were agents of Soviet Russia, and we had gone into Cambodia and Laos in order to get at the Vietnamese, who were agents of the Chinese, who were agents of Soviet Russia. The long chain of argument that explained why America felt compelled to invade Cambodia was invalidated in its first premises when Nixon and Kissinger decided to pursue businesslike relations with Russia and China.

Presumably America's leaders during the Indochina war were aware, for it was often pointed out by scholars, that there was a history of antagonism between China and Vietnam. Vietnam revolted in 39 A.D. and again in 939 A.D. against a Chinese occupation that lasted for a thousand years; and, many wars later, the Vietnamese general who drove a Chinese invading force back across the frontier in 1788 asked how the Chinese, who had invaded Vietnam so often, could remain unaware that the Vietnamese would always drive them out.[11] The leaders of the American government in the 1960s must have known this history, but did not see what it meant. In the American view, historical conflicts are like surface wounds that heal without leaving a scar. Contemporary evidence seemed to show that the Vietnamese communists were under the control of China; and the American government did not appreciate that this alignment was temporary, and that it was caused in large part by the very American actions that were designed to prevent it.

-----

[11]"As Kublai Khan went, so goes Peking," *The Economist*, March 10, 1979, p. 68.

"Tension between China and North Vietnam simmered all during the Vietnam war, but public pronouncements at the time gave little hint of how deep the rift between Peking and Hanoi had become," according to an article that appeared in the New York *Times* in early 1979. The article went on to quote a high official of the Vietnamese government as saying that China had hoped that the American war in Vietnam would go on forever, so that Vietnam would remain dependent on China permanently; the Vietnamese official added that "There was a joke in the Western press during the war that the Chinese would fight to the last Vietnamese. American journalists could have no idea how true that joke was."[12]

From the geopolitical point of view, the American failure in Indochina was not a series of many different blunders; it was a single blunder, but one of epic proportions. It represented a fundamentally mistaken view of what happens, and what forces are at work, in international relations. The American view is that the independence of states has been eroded and the rivalry of states has been muted by the rise of worldwide ideological movements. In the American view, many of the countries of the world have given up nationalism and gone in for larger, more universal causes. The evidence, however, does not support this view.

When Russia, in 1979, threatened to invade China, and when China invaded Vietnam, and when Vietnam invaded Cambodia, it ws demonstrated that these states, although calling themselves communist, were not united and were not one another's puppets. It was to prevent their all becoming part of one Soviet monolith that we involved ourselves in Asian wars for twenty years; and now it looks very much as though, to the extent that they were united even temporarily, it was solely because of our intervention, though our intervention was intended to achieve the opposite effect.

The cost of the American mistake has been staggeringly high.

---

[12]New York *Times*, February 20, 1979, p. A6

In material terms, it cost 150 billion dollars; it induced a ruinous inflation that is with us still; and it depressed confidence in, and the value of, the American dollar. Its social and political costs were higher still: in the 1960s American society fell apart under the impact; Lyndon Johnson's attempt to complete the New Deal had to be abandoned; a generation of Americans grew up to be opponents of their country and its laws; and the rest of the non-communist world lost faith in the United States. The human cost, in Indochinese and American lives, only can be counted but never can be valued. The Indochina war was probably the most costly wrong decision that America has ever made; and it is by no means clear that we will ever fully recover from its effects.

All of this—the lives, the wealth, the country's integrity— were squandered in vain because of a profound and abiding American misunderstanding of international relations. Americans are blind to the fundamental importance of the independence of states, and of the forces that support that independence. We are either unwilling or unable to think about other countries in their own national terms. We basically misunderstand the international politics of the world in which we live.

The Community of Interest

While Americans are the most prone to overestimate the importance of ideological movements, all peoples, and not just Americans, tend to overestimate the effect of alliances upon the independence of states. Especially in wartime alliances, when the differences between allies are subordinated or submerged in the face of a common danger, it is usual to think that a permanent unity has been forged between the allies that transcends the independent ambitions, rivalries, and desires of the particular states. After the war is over, there is disillusionment when the victors quarrel among themselves. The extent of the disarray is par-

ticularly visible when, as in 1815, 1919, and 1945, the united nations that win the war create a permanent organization that is
supposed to maintain the peace.

Even during the effective period of an alliance, differences
between the allies are not so completely forgotten as is usually
supposed. The problem that always faces an alliance was discerned
as early as the fifth century B.C., when the Greek city-states
considered the question of which state should be allowed to lead
them in the war against Persia—for it is axiomatic that any
military force, to be successful, requires a commander, who
makes decisions and gives directions. The Greek word for leader is
"hegemon," and the problem that plagues any alliance is, in a
word, hegemony. The position of leadership is of advantage to
the leader, and the advantage often is used unscrupulously. The
Greek city-states of the fifth century B.C. accepted the leadership
of Athens in the continuing Greek war against Persia, only to find
that they had been duped into becoming part of an Athenian empire, and that the funds that they contributed to the common
alliance were used by Athens for herself.

Nor is the hegemon the only Power that pursues its own individual interests. When the United States entered the Second
World War, the Department of State felt obliged to ask the
Council on Foreign Relations to undertake an extended study of
the claims of America's European allies and of how their claims
related to one another.[13] So numerous were these claims, and so
difficult to reconcile with one another, that the American government needed help just to sort them all out.

An alliance is not a unity; it is an institutionalized diversity, in
which the interests of the allies often are adverse to one another. It
is, for evident reasons, in the interests of an effective alliance to
suppress this truth in order to achieve better unity of action
through greater mutual trust. But states, even when allied, remain independent, and exhibit the characteristics of in-

---

[13]Council on Foreign Relations, *Twenty-Five Years*, p. 18.

dependence. Weaker members of an alliance often complain that the leading country in the alliance is their secret enemy; and, indeed it is instructive as an exercise in looking at things from another point of view to look at an alliance through paranoid eyes and to interpret it, as disaffected members often do, as a plot by its leading state against the other allies, perhaps in tacit complicity with the enemy state against whom the alliance is nominally directed.

Consider, for example, the 1948 Arab war to destroy Israel. The United Nations had decided that, other than the Jerusalem enclave, western Palestine should be partitioned between Jews and Arabs; and that eastern Palestine should become independent as the kingdom of Jordan. Jordan thereupon invaded western Palestine, supposedly to help the proponents of an Arab Palestinian state to destroy the proponents of a Jewish Palestinian state. But in the course of the war, the state that Jordan kept from coming into being, and whose proposed territory it annexed, was not the Jewish state, but the Arab state. Wily King Abdullah of Jordan, it was said, had used the Arab alliance to cloak his own ambitions to conquer fellow Arabs.

In the 1930s, according to some observers, one reason that Chinese warlords were reluctant to accept Generalissimo Chiang Kai-Shek's orders to fight the Japanese was that, if they sent their armies away to the Japanese front, Chiang would occupy their provinces while their armies were away. It was not unreasonable to assume that Chiang was using the war against Japan to distract the attention of independent Chinese provinces from his designs against them.

During the Second World War, General de Gaulle, as his memoirs show, concentrated the greater part of his attention on the struggle against his allies, Britain and the United States. This was not unreasonable, for he lacked the means to contribute significantly to the war against the common enemy. De Gaulle suspected that his allies were plotting to end French dominion over Syria and Lebanon; and the memoirs of the British official charged with the responsibility for these matters indicated that he was working towards exactly that end, although of course he did not think of it as a plot.[14]

French fears that America was plotting against the French position in Indochina were equally well grounded. It now is known that President Roosevelt was determined to prevent a French return to Indochina. Indeed an historian of Roosevelt's foreign policy tells us that Roosevelt planned to abolish the French colonial empire, and that he intended to take Dakar and Indochina from France, and use them both as strategic bases for the United Nations in general "and the United States in particular."[15]

In 1953–54, President Dwight Eisenhower refused to intervene in Indochina on France's behalf, even though the dreaded and hated communists were the enemy; but as soon as France was defeated, the United States moved in and supplanted the French in South Vietnam. To note: the U.S. did not move to take over enemy Communist North Vietnam; the U.S. moved to take over friendly French South Vietnam.

In 1956, President Eisenhower and his Secretary of State, John Foster Dulles, had their opportunity to carry into effect their program of liberating eastern Europe from the Soviet Union, as eastern Europe moved towards revolt. Liberation had been proclaimed, especially by Dulles, to be the purpose of the new administration and of the western alliance; and revolt in eastern Europe put the goal of liberation within grasp. But, in actions that were roughly simultaneous, the United States moved instead against its own allies, Britain and France, in the Suez matter, while Russia, in turn, attacked its ally, Hungary. The real allies seemed to be the U.S.A. and the U.S.S.R.; it was possible to think that they had conspired to split Europe between them and

---

[14]Major-General Sir Edward Spears, *Fulfillment of a Mission: The Spears Mission to Syria and Lebanon, 1941–1944* (Hamden, Connecticut: Archon Books, 1977).
[15]Dallek, *Roosevelt*, p. 460.

that they kept up the fiction of a cold war between them only in order to keep their allies in line. So long as western Europe believed in the reality of a Russian threat it would accept the need for American protection and would therefore have to accept American hegemony. A paranoid might make a plausible case in support of his view that Russia was play-acting its threat for America's benefit, and that America was reciprocating for Russia's benefit.

In 1958, the United States refused de Gaulle's request that France and Britain share in America's directorship of the alliance; while Russia refused China's request to share in the atomic weapons directorate of the communist alliance. There was a parallelism in the twin refusals.

In the late 1960s and early 1970s, in consequence of the Vietnam war, American financial and economic strength declined vis-à-vis her allies in western Europe and Japan. Then, in 1973, the oil cartel, OPEC, declared economic war on the alliance, first by an embargo, and then by a staggering increase in the price of oil. Secretary of State Kissinger proposed to shape a unified alliance strategy to meet the threat, but alliance unity proved difficult to achieve. The governments of allied nations made their individual arrangements with oil-producing countries; and from the point of view of the United States, its allies had let down the alliance by failing to form a common front with America.

Europeans saw things differently. They were puzzled that the United States did not attempt to break up the OPEC cartel; they complained that the American strategy was not easy to understand. But the United States is not so dependent on imported oil as are its chief commercial rivals such as Japan; and in the aftermath of the oil crisis of 1973-74, it became apparent that the economic position of the U.S. as versus its competitors had been significantly strengthened by the crisis. The intimacy between the governments of the United States and of Saudi Arabia, the leader of OPEC, suggested to cynics the possibility that the United States had pretended to oppose the rise in oil prices on behalf of the industrialized world, but in fact had been acting in collusion with Saudi Arabia to push up the price. Secretary Kissinger, after all, proposed to establish a floor under the new high price of oil; and not everybody was prepared to accept his statement that his purpose in doing so was to create an economic situation in which the search for alternative sources of energy would be actively pursued.

The examples could be multiplied, but the point has been made. The value of exploring the paranoid point of view is that it reveals antagonisms that really exist. It helps to show that the creation of an alliance does not destroy the independence of its member states, nor does it necessarily reconcile their conflicting interests. Alliances in international relations are useful and often essential; but their value in terms of unity of sentiment and action is limited to the specific purposes for which, in each case, they are formed. There are conflicts and politics within an alliance; and while the leaders and peoples of each member state may have sincere feelings of loyalty towards their allies, it is the national interest of their own state to which they give priority.

In modern alliances, there is a higher level of functional integration than there used to be in the past. This is true of the North Atlantic Treaty Organization (NATO) as well as of the Warsaw Pact and others. It is instructive in the case even of so integrated a structure to note how the two-way pull works out when alliance interests clash with particular interests of a member state. It is a triumph of alliance interests over individual interests that, for example, NATO makes an attempt to standardize weapons procurement so that the national armed forces of its member states can use the same weapons. On the other hand, member states often lobby to get a weapons system adopted that they themselves manufacture even when their system is more costly or less effective than a weapons system produced by another country. When the commercial interests at stake are sufficiently large, members pursue their own interests rather than those of the alliance as a whole.

The Community of Mankind

Dante has been credited with the view that the division of the human race into fragmented sovereignties is unreal, and that it is the unity of mankind that is real.[16] It always has been the loftiest spirits who have held this point of view; and what invalidates it is that there have been so few of them.

Almost everybody feels at one time or another that one's obligations as a human being ought to come ahead of parochial political loyalties, but on a regular basis nobody puts that feeling into practice. It is so rare for anyone to be willing to risk death for the cause of humanity that Christianity looks back 2,000 years to such an event, and proclaims that He who was willing to be crucified for mankind partook of the nature of God. Yet it is a routine matter, and even a legal duty, for all eligible young male citizens, in time of war, to hazard or offer their lives for their countries.

When it is a question of life or death, the masks come off and the truth is revealed. It is routine and commonplace for everyone to be willing to die for one's country, but almost unheard of for someone to be willing to die for mankind. That is why it is the community of mankind that is the dream—and why it is the world's disunited states that are real.

Should we try to change this situation? Since the continued existence of independent states will mean the renewal of warfare that may destroy the human race, should we not seek to forge the political unity of mankind before it is too late?

---

[16]Martin Wight, "Western Values in International Relations," in Butterfield and Wight, *Diplomatic Investigations*, pp. 89, 92–93.

8

CENTURIES APART

The fact of political fragmentation and the dream of political unity are the poles of discourse in the study of international relations. In the nineteenth century, there were many who would have said that to seek the political unity of mankind would be to go in the wrong direction. In contrast with the nineteenth century, nowadays it is usual to stress the importance of striving towards unity rather than diversity. The dialogue between the points of view representative of the nineteenth and of the twentieth century throws into vivid relief the issue of the direction in which, ideally, international relations ought to be going.

What the Nineteenth Century Said

The nineteenth century is associated with the belief that a diversity of independent states is a desirable state of affairs, and, most important, that each nation should become an independent state.[1] A nation, it was thought, defines itself in terms of a special

---

[1]Many points of view were expressed in the nineteenth century by diverse persons who often (and sometimes violently) disagreed with one another.

mission, and the mission of each was thought to be of value to mankind. The attempt to deprive nations of their independence was a principal cause of international unrest and injustice, so that, in this view, the independence of nations would lead to international harmony and peace.

"In Europe today," wrote Giuseppe Mazzini, who was perhaps the representative revolutionary thinker of the age,

> the word revolution is synonymous with the word nationality. It implies a redrawing of the map of Europe; a cancellation of all treaties based on conquest, compromise, and the wills of reigning houses; a reorganization to be made in line with the temperaments and capabilities of the peoples and with their free consent; a removal of the causes of selfish hostility among the peoples; a balancing of power among them, and therefore the possibility of brotherhood. The sovereignty of that goal must replace the sovereignty of force, caprice and chance.[2]

This was the doctrine of a generous nationalism that asked for other nations the same freedom that it asked for its own nation. It enabled Mazzini, the prophet of Italian nationalism, to inspire the nationalisms of other countries as well. It was in the service of this nationalism that Giuseppe Garibaldi, its greatest hero, fought for Uruguay and for France as well as for Italy, and was offered high command in the army of the American Union during the Civil War; he was the champion of freedom for all peoples, and it is appropriate that, even during the Cold War, his image appeared on the postage stamps of both the U.S. and the U.S.S.R.[3]

What I am discussing is the particular point of view that generally is thought to be distinctive of the age. Similarly, one speaks of the "the Enlightenment" of the eighteenth century although not everybody at that time was enlightened.

[2]Ignazio Silone, ed., *The Living Thoughts of Mazzini* (New York and Toronto: Longmans, Green and Co., 1939), p. 22.

[3]Jasper Ridley, *Garibaldi* (London: Constable, 1974), p. xi.

Victory in the First World War seemingly enabled Woodrow Wilson, Thomas Masaryk, and other proponents of national independence and self-determination to carry this program into effect. The failure of Wilson and his colleagues to establish a peace that was durable has tended to obscure the real merits of the theory that inspired them. Yet the doctrine of national self-determination does have important weaknesses, and they were not irrelevant to the failings of the territorial arrangements made at Versailles.

A basic weakness is that it is difficult to tell what is a nation and what is not. There is no audible or visible manifestation of identity, such as language or color of skin. It is not necessarily a matter of physical location; one child born in Montreal grows up believing himself Canadian, while another grows up believing himself Quebecois. Armenians have lived for nearly three millennia in what is now Turkey, but nobody has ever considered them Turks. Many persons, born and brought up as Christians, who regard themselves as Germans, Frenchmen, or Englishmen, are regarded by their neighbors as Jews, because their parents or ancestors were also regarded as Jews.

Nationhood, dictionaries tell us, basically is defined by common ancestry. The same thing used to be said of the first form of political organization, tribes. The nineteenth-century American anthropologist Lewis Henry Morgan taught that tribes had evolved from families, and his theory was incorporated into the teachings of Woodrow Wilson.[4] It was what the Bible seemed to say on a literal reading; the Children of Israel were in fact the children of a common ancestor named Israel, and as Hebrews, they descended from the eponymous Eber, the ancestor of Abraham. But contemporary anthropology has shown that tribes are formed instead from diverse individuals, attracted by a common leadership.[5] To unify their followers, as King David made a

---

[4]Woodrow Wilson, *The State*, Rev. Ed. (Boston: Heath & Co., 1898), pp. 2–4.

[5]Claude Levi-Strauss, "The Social and Psychological Aspects of Chieftain-

nation out of a dozen Semitic tribes, imaginative leaders create the myth of a common ancestry.

It is this myth that is at the heart of the matter. For the United States, Abraham Lincoln said at Gettysburg: ". . . *our fathers* brought forth upon this continent a nation. . . ." Our fathers; and yet, in literal fact, my own forefathers, and those of vast numbers of other Americans, were at that time an ocean away. What makes us Americans is our willingness to enter into the myth of a common ancestry, and to think about George Washington, Thomas Jefferson, and Alexander Hamilton as though we did indeed come from them. It is also the willingness of those Americans who are literally the descendants of the founding colonists to allow us to participate with them in the common myth.

Thus common ancestry is not an explanation of nationhood; it is instead, an invention that is a manifestation of it. Nationhood remains a mysterious phenomenon. Why it exists is unclear; why it manifests itself differently from nation to nation also is unclear. It is not clear why certain groups have cohered so strongly as to be nearly impervious to the assaults of destiny, while a thousand other nations whose names now are forgotten fell and died at some point along the road. Nor is it clear why the nationalisms of certain groups seem to pose greater problems for the rest of the world than others do. André Malraux, in an interview published ten years ago, chose what for a Frenchman is an obvious example when he remarked that

> the question to be asked is whether Germany is a country in which the idea of the nation seems to be specially dangerous, as, incidentally, it is in all former Fascist countries. The answer is yes. It is harder in Germany than in France to control the national idea. In my view, the problem that faces the German intellectuals is that of how a German na-

---

ship in a Primitive Tribe: The Nambikuara of Northwestern Mato Grosso," in Ronald Cohen and John Middleton, eds., *Comparative Political Systems: Studies in the Politics of Pre-Industrial Societies* (Garden City, New York: The Natural History Press, 1967), p. 45.

tion is to be created that is not the Hitlerian nation. If they are not
prepared to tackle this problem, they are cutting themselves off from
historical development.[6]

What is a nation? To Europeans of the nineteenth and early
twentieth centuries, the answer seemed obvious because there was
widespread agreement as to which groups in Europe were nations.
When an attempt was made to apply the nationality concept to
other continents, however, it became evident that the concept
was vague and its definition elusive. When the statesmen of Versailles turned, for example, from Europe to the restructuring of
the Middle East, it was far from obvious whether the Arabs constituted a single nation, or whether they were several nations, and
if so, what these were. For example, there has been a conflict ever
since the events of 1919–22 about the right to existence of the
four states that emerged from what was then Syria. Even in
Europe, certainties have dissolved, as separatist nationalisms have
emerged in Brittany, Languedoc, the Basque country, Scotland,
and elsewhere.

In other times and places, political entities have been organized
on other bases than that of the national state. City-states, tribes,
dynastic empires, and other such polities have existed and thrived.
Nineteenth-century Europe saw history as a progression from
such political forms towards the ultimate achievement of the
nation-state. The problems of tribal Africa or Arabia thus could
be seen as rites of passage, as they crossed the frontiers of history
from a primitive state to the modern one. Nowadays, though, it is
no longer a common view that history is a progression, or that the
political forms of the past necessarily are inferior to those we have
today.

Nor is it obvious which territory, within which limits, belongs
to each nation, or state, however defined. Mazzini believed that
in a world of independent nations, there would be peace and har-

---

[6]*Encounter,* Vol. xxxii (January 1968), pp. 48–49.

mony if each nation had its own territory and did not covet that of others. But there are nations with rival claims to the same territory, and sometimes there is justification for more than one claimant. Partition or compromise is not always feasible; sometimes, as in western Palestine, a country is arguably too small to hold the two nations that both want to inhabit it. Then there was the case of Armenia, which was to be carved out of the Ottoman empire in 1919; one of the difficulties was that the Armenians were a minority everywhere in the territory that they inhabited, so that self-determination could be given to the Armenians only by denying self-determination to the majority in the territory that would become Armenia. No doubt this was a convenient excuse for going back on the pledges that had been made to the martyred Armenian people, but it also demonstrated the sort of difficulty that arises from an attempt to apply the nationalities principle to a complicated world.

Another difficulty is that, with the passage of time, nations change. Demographic trends suggest that, for example, the central Asian peoples of the Soviet Union are increasing so much more rapidly than the Russians that their claims to independence may one day be taken much more seriously than they are today.

In practice, the political program that calls for each group that believes itself to be a nation to exercise independence in the territory that it regards as its proper homeland leads to conflict more often than it does to harmony.

Nor is this the only problem raised by the theory of national self-determination. Another problem is that it does not allow for the survival of national minorities; for the theory implies that they should either carve out a separatist country of their own, or else leave the country and return to the land of their ancestors. If they are dispersed throughout the country, rather than concentrated in one place, the separatist solution is inapplicable. If the country of their ancestors no longer exists, or does not want to take them back, the second solution is inapplicable too. Presumably the theory of national self-determination in these circumstances requires that national minorities be made to disappear. This illiberal aspect of nationalism was discerned in the nineteenth century by prophetic thinkers such as the Swiss historian Jacob Burckhardt, who warned of its dangers and of its darker side; but it was not until the twentieth century that its terrible consequences were fully manifested.[7]

Thus the Young Turks, when they took control of the Ottoman empire, carried out their program of nationalism by massacres of the Armenian and Greek minorities, who had settled the country two millennia before the coming of the Turks. Similarly Colonel Gamal Abdel Nasser, as the apostle of Arab nationalism, drove from Egypt the Greek community, though it had been there even before the Pharaoh Ahmose II, in the sixth century B.C., established the city of Naukratis in the Nile Delta as a Greek trading post. True, the Greeks had Greece to receive them; true, too, extraterritorial trading posts and treaty ports were hated throughout Asia as a vestige of European colonialism. Yet these were people who had lived in the land for a long time, and who were not at home elsewhere. Modern nationalism made it necessary for many peoples, like the Hebrew tribes in ancient Egypt, to commence an exodus, but it could not promise them a land of their own at the end of the journey, for all the other lands, too, already have been taken.

Throughout the twentieth century, the plight of national minorities in the independent states of nationalist Eurasia has shown that the program of national self-determination leads to tragedy and strife in a world of mixed populations. The program is particularly inappropriate at the present time, because more people than ever before now live, travel, or do business in countries that belong to other peoples.

Another problem that it raises is that not all groups who feel themselves to be nations are large enough to function fully as states in the modern world. We see that with especial force now

---

[7]Jacob Burkhardt, *Force and Freedom: An Interpretation of History,* edited by James Hastings Nichols (New York: Pantheon Books, 1943).

that the European countries are taking leave of their last and weakest colonies, island mini-states too poor in resources to support their present populations, yet unwilling to federate with others to seek strength and prosperity.

There are, in a functional sense, too many states. More than ever, there are issues of regional or worldwide concern, requiring agreement or concerted action by the various states; but the excessive number of states makes negotiations too unwieldy, and brings in too many points of view to be accommodated successfully. Thus arose, from the necessities of the case, a distinction that deprives most states of a full role in international affairs. The term "Great Powers" entered the diplomatic vocabulary in 1814, at Chaumont, where Napoleon's enemies cemented their alliance against him; and its significance was illustrated when the decisions of the Congress of Vienna (1814–15) were made by a committee of the five Great Powers.[8] It was much the same after the First World War, despite Woodrow Wilson's idealism and all of the rhetoric about the rights of small states that had been the stock-in-trade of the allied Powers. At the Paris peace conference, only five Great Powers were permitted to participate at all sessions, and they were the countries that made the terms of the peace settlement.[9] After the Second World War, the victors institutionalized the directorate of the Great Powers, by providing that they should be the five permanent members of the Security Council of the United Nations and that any one of them could veto a decision made by the rest of the Council.

To the extent that the theory of national self-determination called for all nations to participate fully in the political affairs of

---

[8] Harold Nicolson, *The Congress of Vienna: A Study in Allied Unity: 1812-1822* (New York: Harcourt Brace Jovanovich, Inc., A Harbinger Book, 1946), p. 81; Sir Charles Webster, *The Congress of Vienna: 1814-1815* (New York: Barnes & Noble, Inc., 1966), pp. 92–95.

[9] Edwin de Witt Dickinson, *The Equality of States in International Law* (Cambridge: Harvard University Press; London: Oxford University Press, 1920), p. 377.

mankind, it was at odds with the realities of politics. It was un-
workable, and so the expedient of negotiations between the Great
Powers arose to take its place.

Despite all of these failings, the theory of national self-
determination had, and continues to have, considerable value.
One of its merits is that emphasized by the important benefits to
be gained from diversity. For a human being, freedom would
mean considerably less if there were not such a range of political
choices. In this world of diverse social and political systems, to the
extent that governments allow you to come or go, you can choose
to live in a Christian republic or an Islamic kingdom or a socialist
democracy or a socialist dictatorship or a secular free-enterprise
democracy or any one of a number of other combinations. You
can choose for yourself whether to live in a permissive society or a
disciplined one. It is the saving grace of an imperfect world that
beyond the horizon there is someplace different.

For society, too, diversity has an important value, which was
more keenly appreciated, perhaps, in the nineteenth century
than in our own. The theories of evolution and mutation were
fresh in the mind then, with all the many examples of how an
abundance of possibilities and experiments allowed species to
adapt and improve. Biology seemed to confirm the liberal belief
that a variety of opinions best conduces to the discovery of the
truth; and that a variety of alternatives offers the best hope for
development along the best lines.

Aware as we are now of the dangers inherent in political
fragmentation, it may be useful from time to time to remind
ourselves that there are compensating benefits. Mazzini may have
gone too far in saying that every nation has a mission to perform,
but the diverse contributions that the nations make to the world's
political culture do extend the range of political experience and
provide alternatives and options for growth and survival.

Moreover, conflict and competition, more keenly appreciated
in the nineteenth century than today, have positive and important value. These are values that often are lost sight of in today's

world, which, because it is tempestuous, is all the more inclined to value harmony and stability. It may well be that the values of conflict and competition are most important among those that have created human civilization. Certainly many of the inspiring and most significant achievements of mankind have been accomplished under the banners of rival states locked in mortal combat with one another.

The nineteenth-century theory of nationalism tells us, therefore, a good deal about why it is a good thing for the political world to be fragmented rather than unified. In addition it tells us that, whether fragmentation along national lines is good or bad, it corresponds with the aspirations of people everywhere; and in this respect the theory of nationalism provides us with a key to political understanding as we observe the course of world political events even today.

Quite rightly, the theory of nationalism identifies the denial of national independence as a persistent cause of discord and discontent. It also identifies nationalist sentiment as the most important moving force in international politics; and here again it has been proven right time and again. General de Gaulle saw so clearly what was happening and what was going to happen in international affairs because he looked upon Russia and China, for example, as states, and therefore as potential rivals, while a succession of American administrations misperceived the two great Powers as a communist monolith that had left nationalism far behind.

The nineteenth-century theory of nationalism accordingly has provided the key to an understanding of international politics even in the twentieth century. Of the states of Latin America, Africa, and Asia, Professor Stanley Hoffmann has written perceptively that, "Our nineteenth century is very much their twentieth, and consequently their view of order is unlikely to be the same as ours. It is often less concerned with long-term problems . . . than with the achievement of power and autonomy."[10] In other words, the concerns of the overwhelming majority of countries today are best described in terms of the nineteenth-century theory of nationalism. The intellectual leaders of the advanced industrial states think in terms that go beyond nationalism, but it is by no means clear that even their countrymen share these post-nationalist concerns.

What the Twentieth Century Says

In the twentieth century, large numbers of people have come to believe that the consequences of the scientific and industrial revolution have made the political fragmentation of the world dangerously obsolete.

The arguments supporting this conclusion are by now familiar, and need not be repeated here in any great detail. Weapons of mass destruction have made warfare so dangerous that it might bring about the end of the world; and since warfare is inevitable in a world of multiple sovereignties, the political structure of the world must be unified. The environmental impact of modern technology is so great that peacetime activities, too, must be regulated on a worldwide basis. Resources in scarce supply must be phased out and replaced on a planned basis. The monetary and other economic affairs of the industrialized nations are so intertwined that, without central coordination, there will be chaos and collapse.

Thus the objective realities of the modern world, stemming from the scientific-technical-industrial revolution, rationally require the establishment of a worldwide political authority; but

---

[10]Stanley Hoffmann, *Primacy or World Order: American Foreign Policy Since the Cold War* (New York: McGraw-Hill Book Company, 1978), p. 139.

131

the subjective, or political, realities stubbornly resist such a conclusion, and there is no reason to believe that these political
realities will disappear in the foreseeable future. A great deal of
wishfulness has gone into the often-heard proposition that the in-
creased interdependence and fragility of the world has caused an
erosion of national sovereignty. Perhaps it is something that
ought to have happened, but it has not happened. There is a
great deal of cooperation at all economic, social, and political
levels between America and the other non-communist industrialized nations; but in the first place these are allies, sharing
a certain number of common goals and to some extent a common
culture, and in the second place, times are essentially prosperous,
so there is little reason for discord. Where important national interests clash, each nation still goes its own way. It is true that
governments nowadays are involved in such rational and non-
political activities as business, science, and management; but the
result is not that government has become rationalized and non-
political, but that business, science, and management have been
politicized.

These are among the many reasons for dissenting from the
prevalent view among international relations scholars today, ex-
emplified by the work of Robert Keohane and Joseph Nye, that
an analysis of the inter-relations of independent states no longer
provides an adequate explanation for much of what is happening
in a changing world.[11] For example, they say, the priority given to
national security questions—a priority typical of inter-state relations—is giving way to questions of "low politics" such as economic and social policy, so that even Secretary of State Henry
Kissinger abandoned his preoccupation with traditional diplomatic issues in 1973 in order to focus on the question of oil.[12]
They miss the point. Secretary Kissinger took up the ques-

---

[11]Robert O. Keohane and Joseph S. Nye, *Power and Interdependence:
World Politics in Transition* (Boston and Toronto: Little, Brown and Company, 1977), p. vii.

[12]Keohane and Nye, *Interdependence*, pp. 23–25.

tion of oil because it *had become* a national security issue. The same is true of the other economic and social issues which are now so high on the list of foreign policy priorities.

Another proposition that they advance is that states are being shouldered aside by other actors on the world stage; but that does not seem to be true either. It was in centuries long past that non-state actors played so great a role; not merely the Papacy, in the days when it was a dominating factor in world politics, capable of bringing the Holy Roman emperor himself to his knees at Canossa, but also business corporations such as the East India Company which commanded armies and empires, and private individuals like Cecil Rhodes who carved out and conquered territories in sovereign style. It is no longer so. Today it is no longer a businessman like Sir Henri Deterding or John D. Rockefeller who controls a major share of the world's oil supplies; it is the cartel of state governments called OPEC. It is not a Basil Zaharoff who sells armaments to the world; it is the government of the United States, or France, or Czechoslovakia. Economic interests have not taken over from the governments; on the contrary, governments have taken over the economic interests. The scholars of international relations seem to live in a world of their own, which the businessmen and lawyers who deal with these matters on a regular basis would not recognize as bearing much resemblance to daily reality. An article in a recent issue of a journal devoted to law and business begins with the sentence, "Today more than at any time in history, foreign states, and their agencies and instrumentalities, are engaged in activities traditionally performed by private parties that directly affect trade and commerce."[13] It is a statement so observably true that it is hard to imagine why anyone would deny it.

---

[13]James Hugo Friend, "Suing a Foreign Government Under the United States Antitrust Laws: The Need for Clarification of the Commerical Activity Exception to the Foreign Sovereign Immunities Act of 1976," *Northwestern Journal of International Law and Business*, Vol. 1 (Autumn 1979), p. 657.

THE INDEPENDENCE OF NATIONS

It is equally hard to imagine why Keohane and Nye think that "the recourse to force seems less likely now" than it was in the century before 1945.[14] It was after, and not before, 1945 that such destructive wars took place as the French colonial struggles in Indochina and Algeria, the American crusades in Korea and Indochina, the near-genocidal battles of Cambodia, and the never-ending wars between Israel and her neighbors. It was after 1945, too, that international terrorism emerged full-scale to attack airlines and embassies all around the world and add a new dimension to the use of force in world politics.

In what they describe as a world of complex interdependence, Keohane and Nye see political bargaining as the process that has replaced the use of force.[15] E. H. Carr hoped for the same thing in 1939; he drew an analogy with the bargaining process that takes place in industrial disputes between unions and management.[16] Hitler did not bargain with Poland in 1939; his armies invaded her. Russia, in 1979 and thereafter, did not bargain with Afghanistan; it invaded, occupied, and suppressed, as Warsaw Pact forces had done in Hungary in 1956 and in Czechoslovakia in 1968. The overly optimistic views of representative thinkers of the twentieth century indicate a failure to understand political reality; the persistence in maintaining these views, even after events time and again have shown them to be false, seems to indicate a certain amount of unwillingness to make the attempt.

Keohane and Nye (and I return to them again because of their outstanding qualities as originators and expositors of advanced twentieth-century views) argue that realism (which is to say, Hans Morgenthau's views, and such views as I have advanced in these pages) represents an ideal type or model, and that the complex interdependence that they describe represents an alternative model; and that neither realism nor interdependence represents the world as it actually is, but that sometimes one and sometimes the

---

[14]Keohane and Nye, *Interdependence*, p. 28.
[15]Keohane and Nye, *Interdependence*, p. 11.
[16]Carr, *Crisis*, pp. 269–272.

other provides a better explanation of what goes on in the real world. Such is the central thesis that they propose. It is an academic approach, in line with thinking in the social sciences (since Max Weber) in making use of the ideal type or model. One of the several ways in which it errs is in mistaking the realist interpretation of world politics for a model. It is not intended to be one.

I do not say, as a model-builder would, that the world always is at war; and then say that, when wars do take place, the real world temporarily is well explained by my model of perpetual war. On the contrary, I believe peace to be as real and as temporary as war. In the world in which we live, I see more cooperation between countries than there has ever been before, and more competition. I see more of everything: more people, more countries, and more contacts and relationships of every sort between them. My endeavor is to explain what underlies it all — to explain, in other words, what, in international relations, is fundamental. It is an aspect of the fundamental truth, as I conceive it to be, that whenever the tangled web of cooperative and competitive international dealings breaks down in an irreconcilable conflict, the issue tends ultimately to be decided by warfare, whereas in domestic politics it would be decided by litigation or legislation. I regard this as a statement, not about the ideal, but about the real.

Even within their own model-building terms, the Keohane and Nye thesis does not hold up, and it is a tribute to their mischievous brilliance that they have persuaded their colleagues that it does. It will be recalled that, of the two models they describe, the realism of Morgenthau, as versus their own "complex interdependence," they claim that sometimes one best explains world politics and sometimes the other. On the contrary: these "models" are not of equally general applicability, for one of them is not of general applicability at all. Hans Morgenthau, George Kennan, Raymond Aron, Georg Schwarzenberger, and other realists have supplied, in their works, examples drawn from the history of many countries and centuries to validate their views.

135

In effect, they have presented the history of the world as evidence to support the realist explanation. For their own part, Keohane and Nye present only two issues and U.S. relations with only two countries as examples of what can be explained by complex interdependence; and they concede that the explanation does not perfectly fit even the two issues that they have selected, and that the two countries they discuss are special cases from which generalizations cannot validly be drawn.

It is as if someone had come upon a rare medical report of a human baby born with two heads, and thereupon had formulated a thesis according to which there are two equally valid ideal descriptions of human beings, one being more appropriate in some cases and the other in others, the two descriptions being that (1) all human beings are born with one head, and (2) all human beings are born with two heads. In fact, the one statement asserts a rule and the other an exception to it; they are therefore not both statements of a general rule.

Keohane and Nye's complex interdependence remains an ideal without general application to today's world; and it does so even though the authors correctly claim that there is a transnational elite that believes in it. In the non-communist industrial countries, for example, there is a class of scientists, industrial managers, and computer specialists who regard national frontiers as artificial and whose view is that scientific, technical, and economic facts are more important than political facts. But unlike the aristocracy of old Europe, which also was a transnational elite, they are not even in power and in a position to translate their views into policy. That theirs may be the right way does not guarantee that it is the path that will be taken by those who exercise power, or by the nationalistic masses from whom ultimately power flows.

On the contrary: on our small, frightened, misguided planet we spend a million dollars *a minute* on armaments—while a billion people go to bed hungry every night.[17]

---

[17]TRB, "A Bigger Bang," *The New Republic*, May 27, 1978, p. 2.

The theory that what is rational necessarily will be done, and that what is irrational necessarily not be done, is contradicted by history and everyday experience. It is a view that ignores the realities of human nature and of group behavior. Seventy years ago, in one of the most famous books of the twentieth century, *The Great Illusion,* Norman Angell showed that, in economic terms, war and imperialism do not pay; yet nations continued, and still continue, to go to war, and to fight to keep their empires. As an analysis of the factors at work in world politics, the view that nationalism has lost its force repeatedly has been shown to be false.

It is true that the world has changed in such a way that now, to a certain extent, we are all in the same boat. For whatever reason, it was in the 1930s that this first seemed to become generally clear. Not merely in the political writings of the period, but also in its imaginative literature, one finds an expression of the perception that all of us are affected even by events that occur far away in time or place. On the opening page of his novel *Look Homeward, Angel,* Thomas Wolfe wrote that "our lives are haunted by a Georgia slattern, because a London cutpurse went unhung." He wrote that "Each of us is all the sums he has not counted; subtract us into nakedness and night again, and you shall see begin in Crete four thousand years ago the love that ended yesterday in Texas." In *For Whom the Bell Tolls,* Ernest Hemingway took his title and his opening quotation from the lines in which John Donne affirmed that "No man is an island" and that "any man's death diminishes me, because I am involved in mankind." The inference frequently drawn was that all should draw together to seek collective security against the dark forces that then threatened mankind. Apart from a few brave individuals, however, people waited until their own interests or frontiers were attacked before joining in the common defense.

H. G. Wells described with great clarity what was responsible for this situation in which we seem to be affected in important ways by what happens to one another. Writing in 1931, to predict

137

what the world would be like in 1981, he warned that

> All contemporary governments have been outgrown—physically and mentally—by the needs of mankind. The abolition of distance, foretold 50 years ago, is achieved. That has made all the governments in the world misfits. Seventy-odd sovereign governments, all acting independently and competitively, all jammed together by that abolition of distance, are trying to carry on the affairs of our race, which now, under the new conditions, would be far more conveniently and successfully dealt with as one world business.[18]

Yet instead of moving in the rational direction, toward one central government, history in the years since H. G. Wells wrote those lines has taken exactly the opposite course, so that instead of being ruled by 70 governments, we now are ruled by closer to 170. Thus world politics are driving in one direction while the oncoming requirements of the scientific revolution of our time are approaching in the same lane but are headed in the opposite direction. This places mankind on a collision course with destiny; so that the ultimate questions in international politics, to which we now must turn, are why the human race has moved in the direction that it has, and whether its course can or should be changed.

---

[18]H. G. Wells, "What Will This World Be Like Fifty Years From Now?" reprinted in London in *The Observer*, December 28, 1980, p. 17.

9

ALEXANDER'S PATH, AND OURS

The criterion by which, above all, we have come to judge long-term directions in world politics is whether they eventually will lead to the abolition of warfare. A related criterion is whether they will lead to a situation in which other matters of global concern also will be dealt with on the basis of a planetary overview. There are several alternative approaches toward the achievement of these ends, and they will be discussed presently.

To the men and women of prior ages, these criteria would have appeared fanciful. Warfare, like disease and poverty, always has appeared to be in the nature of things. It has seemed to be one of the harsh but unavoidable terms of the human political condition. In part, our refusal to accept it is one more manifestation of the twentieth-century revolt against the notion of the inevitable. It is one of the special characteristics of our time. It is something that can be heard in John Maynard Keynes's prediction that the struggle for subsistence, which always has been the primary problem of the human race, can be solved permanently within a hundred years.[1] It is something that can be felt in medical

---

[1]John Maynard Keynes, *Essays in Persuasion* (New York: Harcourt Brace and Company, 1932), p. 366.

research aimed at slowing or halting altogether the process of aging in human beings, and that can be seen in the mission of the astronauts who fly off to the moon and whose name proclaims a wish to go on to the stars. In terms of world politics, it expresses itself in the belief that escape is possible from the trajectory of history, and that the old imperatives no longer need to be obeyed.

There is more to our refusal of acceptance in this area, though, than one more manifestation of the spirit of revolt. The refusal to accept the inevitability of warfare occupies a special place in the thought and feeling of the twentieth century. It was the result of a process somewhat analagous to a religious conversion, in which the masses of the people suddenly are swept by belief in a message of prophecy to which previously they had lent deaf ears. The profound shock of recognizing what warfare had become in modern times forced them finally to listen, and to seek out the truth.

They went about it in a way as old as the Homeric poems. When the wandering Ulysses sought counsel as to how to find his way, he dug a trench, spilled the blood of sacrifices into it, and, when he had thus roused up a ghostly prophet from the underworld, he fed him with more blood in return for a true vision — a terrible vision — of where the voyage was headed. In the odyssey of the modern world, it happened in the blood-soaked trenches of the First World War. The sacrifices purchased a view of what lies ahead.

What lies ahead, if basic changes are not made in world politics, is the eventual destruction of the human race through warfare. An important achievement of the generation that emerged from the victories o the 1914 war was that they understood this and communicated it to succeeding generations; but that was the limit of their achievement. They did not have an understanding of the nature of the politics they proposed to change, and they did not have an effective program for making the fundamental changes that they said were needed.

The initial question, which they failed to adequately consider, was whether their objectives could be accomplished in a world of independent sovereign states, or whether their accomplishment required the establishment of a single world state. The answer given by statesmen throughout the twentieth century, and embodied in the League of Nations, the Kellogg-Briand Pact to outlaw war, and the United Nations is that it can be done in a world of independent sovereign states. Events have discredited that answer.

Woodrow Wilson and the other proponents of the now discredited view did not see the inconsistency between their espousal of world order and their espousal of national self-determination. Theirs was a program that could work only if the nations always were in agreement; for since the nations were free to go their own way, they would do so whenever they disagreed.

The Nature of International Politics

Wilson and his colleagues claimed that there had to be a complete break with traditional patterns of international relations, and particularly with balance-of-power politics and with the use of war as an instrument of national policy. They proposed to abandon the traditional tools of international politics, but did not offer any effective new tools with which to replace them. It is no wonder that their program failed.

They misunderstood the nature of international politics. Oddly enough, so did their critics. E. H. Carr is the most brilliant example of a critic of Wilsonian idealism who saw that it was a failure, but then went on to misunderstand the nature of the failure. Carr claimed that the world has a political society, but that in the 1930s, when he wrote his book, that society had been breaking down and had entered into a state of crisis. The flaw was in his premise: the world, as such lacks a political society; the system does not function because it does not exist.

Those who write about inter-state relations today fall into a

141

similar error: they employ political-science words and concepts derived from the study of how a group or a society functions to describe how independent states behave. To be a state is to belong to a category, not to a group. There is no family of nations, because nations do not have families. There is no society of states, because a society is a group of human beings; no worldwide political society of which the inhabitants of the various states are members, because the peoples of the world have not joined together to achieve a program of common political goals. There are regional cultures in which the inhabitants of certain nations hold a common membership, but in case of conflict, it is the political loyalty to the separate state, not the loyalty to the common culture, that prevails. The state has no effective rivals, for although multinational corporations, labor unions, and administrative agencies are often referred to as new actors on the world stage, they do not attract the primary political loyalty of peoples anywhere.

Commercial and other activities do take place on a global scale, but they are not regulated on a global scale. The now-familiar questions that this raises are how states can deal with one another on a continuing basis, and how transnational economic, social, and cultural activities can continue to grow in importance in a world lacking an overall authority to make and enforce rules. In the past, these continuous dealings did not take place on so vast and important a scale that the need for such an authority was felt to be urgent. Now it is. The interconnection of the world's economies and systems has made modern civilization fragile. Our technological networks are vulnerable, and their disruption can have devastating effects. In the context of international relations, interdependence invites conquest of one by the other, while vulnerability invites exploitation by the blackmail of terrorism.

The threat of invasion and conquest is an old problem, but terrorism is a modern one.[2] Terrorism, which is a pollution of the

---

[2]David Fromkin, "The Strategy of Terrorism," *Foreign Affairs*, Vol. 53 (July 1975), p. 683.

political process, is a close relative to the pollution of the global environment in that both are problems that have gone out of control in the twentieth century: no state is big enough to deal with them on its own, and states will not deal with them by combining because the perceived interests of the various states are too often opposed to one another.

The prognosis for a world that is so vulnerable is that it will suffer from painful and frequent disruptions. In the short run, the world must learn how to live with disruption. Business and labor will have to make greater allowance for the increasing cost of insurance against risk. Individuals will have to adjust their expectations to allow for breakdowns. Governments in their dealings with one another more than ever will have to temper ambitions and beliefs with a prudent regard for international balance and stability; they may have to pursue programs that are likely to appear second-best, but with which other governments are prepared to cooperate, rather than go it alone in pursuit of programs they prefer.

What I have described thus far is not domestic politics gone wrong; it is a different kind of politics altogether. It is unlike every other kind of politics that the human race has developed. International relations are *sui generis*. The thesis of this book is that, because they are rooted in the independence of corporate entities, international politics are fundamentally different, and must be understood and conducted in their own terms.

The Old Politics and the New

International politics take place in a state of anarchy. Anarchy literally means an absence of government, but it does not necessarily mean chaos. What it does mean is that nobody is in charge; but a certain amount of stability can be achieved nonetheless, if the leaders of the independent states act with a certain amount of prudence and intelligence.

At its best, the creative statesmanship of the nineteenth century showed how much can be accomplished along these lines. Talleyrand, Bismarck, and Salisbury pursued foreign policies that advanced the interests of their respective countries, but at the same time they placed limits on how far they thought the power of their countries ought to be expanded. All of them recognized that immoderate power is a danger even to the country possessing it. Their successful pursuit of political equilibrium gave Europe, in the century from 1815 to 1914, peace and stability such as few civilizations have enjoyed.

Their record compares favorably with our own. The twentieth century has been violent, disorderly, and bloody on an unparalleled scale. History does not allow a comparison of records on a conclusive basis, because the circumstances in which nineteenth-century statesmen succeeded were radically different from those in which twentieth-century statemen have failed. Yet there is reason to believe that it was a change in political approach that made at least some of the difference between success and failure. In the old politics, balance was the aim, and war and the threat of war were used, where necessary, to achieve it. In the new politics ushered in by Woodrow Wilson and his colleagues, unity of action was the aim, and war and the threat of it were renounced as instruments of national policy. When Hitler came to power in Germany and immediately embarked on a program of challenging the existing power relationships and of violating Germany's commitments under the Versailles treaty, the old politics called for British and French intervention against his regime. There is little doubt that, at least until 1936, intervention by the allied Powers could easily have overwhelmed Germany and destroyed the Hitler regime. Britain and France, however, followed the dictates of the new politics. Since they could not agree to act together, neither acted; and since they could not threaten to go to war, they allowed Hitler to succeed in every bluff. Their policy of peace at any price strengthened the Hitler regime at home and abroad, and whetted its appetite for further conquests.

144

Thus their unwillingness to go to war led to the outbreak of the Second World War and to all of the horrors that then ensued.

If the old politics were so much more effective, then why did they, too, break down, as they did in 1914? One answer is that their dictates no longer were followed by the leaders of the principal European states. In Germany, Bismarck was dismissed from office, and his successors pursued the immoderate ambitions against which he had warned. Britain, meanwhile, allowed herself economically and militarily to decay. It was not the balance of power, but the erosion of the balance, that led to the outbreak of the 1914 war.

Perhaps the more important answer, however, is that in the end, whenever that might be, the balance of power always breaks down. It is a vice inherent in multiple sovereignties that each country, in acting to fulfill its own legitimately felt security needs, takes the risk that in doing so it will breed some measure of fear and insecurity in neighboring countries. At some point, that insecurity tends to find violent expression. The First World War need not have occurred as early as 1914, and had Bismarck's successors been as wise as Bismarck, it would not have occurred for a long time thereafter; but at some point it, or some war like it, inevitably would have been fought because wars are the way in which a world of multiple sovereignties transacts its basic business.

The old politics brought orderliness, stability, and peace much, but not all, of the time. They have been rejected by leaders of the Western Powers throughout the twentieth century because of the valid perception that modern weapons might make even one more major war fatal to the human race. What is obviously needed is a kind of politics that will bring orderliness, stability, and peace all of the time. In an attempt to find such a kind of politics, we have rejected the old politics, which worked a good deal of the time, in favor of new politics that do not work at all.

The Questions Answered

Unrealistic expectations about what can be achieved in a world of multiple sovereignties are responsible for many of the policy failures of twentieth-century statesmanship, as well as for the intellectual failures that lead students of international relations to continue to puzzle over questions that are not really difficult to answer once it is recognized that the emperor is not wearing any clothes. Thus E. H. Carr and his colleagues wondered why, in international affairs, power factors play so great a role; but once we understand that world politics are fundamentally different from other kinds of politics, we can see that there is nothing about it that should cause wonder. In world politics, power is not restrained because no worldwide authority exists to restrain it. In such circumstances it would be puzzling only if power factors were *not* predominant.

Another question is the one posed by Henry James in the letter quoted in Chapter 1: how mankind could have seemed to have advanced so far towards civilization when, in the light of subsequent wartime behavior, we instead seem to have remained so close to barbarism. The answer is that we have achieved civilization within states but not between them. Henry Adams, who in 1904 thought that the foreign policy America then pursued held out so much promise for the world that "For the first time in fifteen hundred years a true Roman *pax* was in sight. . . ," saw a possibility that if he and his friends could return to the earth in 1938, perhaps, "for the first time since man began his education among the carnivores, they would find a world that sensitive and timid natures could regard without a shudder."[3] In 1938, they in fact would have arrived just in time to witness the dying gasps of the Spanish Republic, Nazi Germany's annexation of Austria, and the craven surrender of Britain and France to Hitler at

---

[3]Henry Adams, *The Education of Henry Adams: An Autobiography* (Boston and New York: Houghton and Mifflin Company, The Riverside Press, Cambridge, 1918), pp. 503, 505.

Munich—hardly the ideal world for sensitive and timid natures. The optimistic view of the future typified by Adams therefore may have seemed to have been invalidated by events. But that was not entirely true. Had he returned in 1938, Adams would have found that his country, although still in the grip of a terrible economic depression, had developed a belief in the responsibility of the community as a whole for the sheltering and welfare of each of its citizens; and he might well have seen in this an advance towards civilized values. He would have seen that his optimism was justified with respect to one kind of politics but not with respect to another.

The basic question is why this is so, why the values that can be realized in national politics are not realized in global politics. Conditioned by success at home in moving toward justice, welfare, and stability, the public asks why there is no noticeable movement toward these goals in the world at large. The question is asked because the state and its achievements are so taken for granted that its goals and accomplishments are wrongly thought to be phenomena that are natural. They are not natural; they are, in the best sense of the word, artificial.

The state is a work of art. It expresses values that are uniquely human. Entering into a universe where strength prevails, where the weak suffer, and where the wounded are left to die, the human race has invented notions of justice and mercy and moral purpose, and has created a multitude of political societies within which such notions are interpreted and realized. It is land reclaimed from the sea; and these notions are dikes manned against the impersonal tides of the universe.

The state is so well established that its assumptions and conditions are forgotten. Generations of scholars have puzzled over the question of why there is war, when they should have been considering the question of why, in domestic politics, there usually is peace. What ought to have been the subject of wonder was the rise of conscience and the consequent growth of order and justice within human societies. In Great Britain, for example, the expan-

147

sion of the King's Peace from the king's physical presence, first to his highways, and then to the whole kingdom, and the concomitant development of the common law, provide an illustration, at which one might marvel, of the process by which justice is created out of chaos and disorder.

Peace, justice, and similar human values are internal manifestations of states because they must be *made* to happen; and states can make things happen only within the ambit of their power. If the world had a ruler whose power embraced the whole globe, he might prevent the states of the earth from fighting one another; the reason that countries continue to wage war against one another is that there is no such ruler to keep them from doing so.

The twentieth-century perception that mankind cannot afford to continue waging wars, and the related perception that changes in circumstances such as the growth of a world economy also require the institution of a single global authority, force the conclusion that a world state and a world government must be created. Nonetheless, governments and peoples have not moved in this direction. They have moved in the opposite direction by dividing and subdividing into an increasingly large number of independent states, and separatist movements throughout the world seem likely to cause the trend to continue.

It is not so much that governments and peoples have failed to understand the new imperatives of life in the nuclear age; it is that human behavior is not governed entirely by rational considerations, and that even when acting rationally, human beings do not always take the long view. What is remarkable, then, is not how little, but how much governments and peoples have demonstrated their awareness that modern conditions require important changes in political processes and conduct. The proliferation of international technical, social, and economic agencies; the extent of international cooperation and consultation in matters ranging from currency regulation to environmental protection; and the daily contacts between representatives of all the world's governments would all appear astounding examples of enlightened and even altruistic conduct to an observer from an earlier age. There are numerous instances of contemporary governments taking the large view and acting responsibly. But it is not the least surprising that they do not do so all the time, and that when such behavior runs counter to their important interests, they do not do so at all.

Alexander, and the Road to World Order

The only way in which decisions regularly might be based on what is best for the planet as a whole would be if such decisions were made by a world government. World government offers the one possibility of creating a just and orderly world without warfare.

On what basis might such a government be established? If they were serious about their goals, this is the question with which the survivors of the 1914 war ought to have been grappling. One of their contemporaries undertook the task with great distinction. It was the British classical scholar W.W. Tarn who explained one of the two views about the requirements of world government in terms of what Alexander the Great may have said at a ceremony of reconciliation with his troops.[4] The ceremony took place at Opis, in the middle of Asia, some 2,300 years ago, at the end of Alexander's career of conquest and shortly before his death. Before the 9,000 soldiers who were his guests, Alexander said a prayer over the loving-cup that held the wine mixture that he and, symbolically, all of his guests were to share. It is not known with any certainty what he said. Tarn attempted to identify the main strands of thought that went into the prayer in a way that was relevant not only to Alexander's world but also to the world that had been shattered by the First World War. Alexander, according to

---

[4]W. W. Tarn, *Alexander the Great*, 2 vols. (Cambridge, London, New York, and Melbourne: Cambridge University Press, 1948), Vol. 1, pp. 115–118; Vol. 2, pp.434–449.

Tarn, prayed for peace, asserted that all men were sons of one Father, and said that he himself had been trusted by God with a mission to act as the Reconciler of the World. The metaphor by means of which he explained how he would accomplish his mission was drawn from the loving-cup: he would mix together all the peoples of the world even as the wines were mixed in the loving-cup, until they became one. Tarn, despite his admiration for his hero, doubted whether even Alexander could have done it. Other historians have doubted whether Alexander even said it; but whether he did so or not, the analysis that Tarn attributed to him is both profound and important.

Tarn's Alexander in effect said that even a world government could not succeed except in the context of a world nation. Alexander, before he arrived at Opis, already had established what in terms of his world was a world government. He ruled almost all of the known world. Yet he said that even his rule could not bring peace unless his subjects were to become one people.

He went further, and said they would have to become one people by mixing together until they were the same. Ethnic, linguistic, religious, and other differences would have to disappear, presumably through intermarriage.

It seems to be an impossible program to realize. If Tarn's Alexander was correct in suggesting that it is the necessary prerequisite of successful world government, then it would seem that world government never can succeed, not even in the most distant future. This is one of the points made by the author of the article on warfare in the 1929 edition of the *Encyclopaedia Britannica*, who wrote that ". . . war is the outcome of the growth of societies which can never be uniform. . . . No super-State can prevent this diversity nor repress the expansion of a vigorous community. The establishment of a world-State would no doubt be the end of international wars, but they would reappear as civil wars."[5]

The other, and more usual, point of view is that a world state, and even a world nation, can be fashioned out of diverse groups.

---

[5]*Encyclopaedia Britannica,* 11th Ed., s.v. "War."

It is something that tends to be assumed rather than argued. It rests on the observation that the United States, the Soviet Union, and the other countries of the world were forged from diverse groups that, in many cases, remain diverse. Failing to make the distinction between world politics and other kinds of politics, it draws the false conclusion that a successful world state necessarily could be created in the same sort of way.

Perhaps the world can be politically unified, but if so it probably will have to be done on a basis different from that on which today's independent countries were unified. The reason lies at the heart of the difference between world politics and other kinds of politics. World politics are not based on patterns of thought; for if they had been, the persuasive argument that human survival requires global unity would have had a greater impact on the direction of events. They are based instead on patterns established at a deeper level. The independence of nations is an expression of the loyalty of populations, and reflects instinctive patterns of human behavior that seem to go back to the origin of the human race.

The Psychological Basis of World Politics

The nature of the behavior patterns underlying world politics is suggested by recent experiments with a group of teenage boys: when divided into groups on a random basis, those who were assigned to one group would begin to discriminate against members of the other groups.[6] The important point to note is that they were divided randomly. Had they been divided on the basis of some characteristic they shared in common, it would have been different. Had one group consisted of all the tall boys while the other consisted of all the shorter ones, it could have been argued that the tall boys feel proud, and the shorter boys defensive about their height, and that this provides an explanation of

---

[6]Henry Tajfel, "Experiments in Intergroup Discrimination," *Scientific American*, Vol. 223 (November 1970), p. 96.

why the two groups discriminated against one another. In these experiments, however, since the basis of selection for each group was entirely random, the discrimination practiced by members of each group against members of the others resulted solely from the fact of membership in a group.

Gibbon, Procopius, and other historians concerned with the later Roman Empire provide a vivid illustration of how this process works in political life in their accounts of the circus and hippodrome factions in ancient Rome and Constantinople. Chariot racers at that time wore colors of red, white, green, or blue; and at some point the backers of the racers began to arrange themselves into factions, distinguished by the color of the racer whom they were backing. The conflict that developed between these factions grew to such proportions that it shook the foundations of government, family, and society. Religious and political significance was read into the choice of one color or the other and caused the feuds to become bloodier. Sedition and blasphemy were imputed by those who favored one color to those who favored another. Gibbon writes that on the occasion of one religious festival, the Greens massacred three thousand Blues; and that at another point, the Blues took control of Constantinople and indulged in a bloody orgy of persecution of the Greens that included mass execution.[7] It was only the higher loyalty that all of them owed to Rome and Byzantium that eventually kept the conflict within bounds. In "the blind ardour of the Roman people, who devoted their lives and fortunes to the colour which they had espoused," one sees an extreme example of what effect membership in a group has on its members.[8]

Why Wars Are Fought

One sees, too, that the ostensible cause of conflict between groups

---

[7]Edward Gibbon, *The Decline and Fall of the Roman Empire*, Chapter XL.
[8]*Ibid.*

need not be of any great importance. This relates to the many modern theories according to which warfare can be eliminated by resolving certain particular economic, social, or political issues. Frederick Schuman's belief that war arises from the greed of the ruling classes leads to the Marxist prescription of a classless society as the guarantor of perpetual peace. E. H. Carr presciently singled out the struggle for control of scarce natural resources, and the inequality of wealth between countries, as the reasons that wars would continue to be fought; and a half-century after he wrote, the international cartel of oil-producing states, OPEC, and the group of poorer countries largely in the southern hemisphere indeed have placed these issues high on the agenda of world politics. They are genuinely important questions, and not mere pretexts for conflict. But it is not so much issues that cause wars; it is the context in which the issues arise. In the mutually discriminatory atmosphere of international relations, issues that otherwise would be peacefully resolved can flare out of control. Putting it the other way around, resolving the important issues in international politics would not lead to perpetual peace; if important issues were unavailable, countries nonetheless from time to time would fight each other about trivial ones.

This is not always apparent because the disputes in which we ourselves are involved usually seem to us to be so important. Time and distance give us the perspective to see the relative unimportance of the issues at stake in many of yesterday's conflicts, and it seems likely that posterity will view at least some of ours in the same way. As we sit, spectators in today's arena, the battle between the partisans of the Green and the Blue chariot teams may seem important enough, but it will become too dark to see the difference between one color and the other once the night of history falls.

Resolving important specific issues, however desirable it may be to do so in other respects, will not solve the general problem caused by the inevitability of at least some amount of warfare in a world of independent states. This is all the more true today as

153

growing nationalism deepens and intensifies the differences between countries.

The Other Side of Patriotism

Creating a world government indeed might have been an easier undertaking centuries ago, when the world needed it less, than it is now when the world needs it more. At a time when rulers had little to do with their subjects, who were often foreign; when lands and populations were acquired by marriage or inheritance, and were treated like private estates rather than countries; and when one ruler might be lord of several domains, widely separated by land or sea, populations had little sense of membership in the kingdoms or empires to which they belonged. The development of the national state in modern times has changed all that, as has the development of effective modern means of communication such as television that can be used and controlled by national governments. The result has been the development of a sense of common membership in political communities and therefore of intense national patriotism.

The growing strength of nationalism displays the complementary aspects of loyalty and discrimination: loyalty to one's own group expressed by discrimination against the members of others. The savagery of twentieth-century politics and warfare often has been explained on the basis of one theory or another according to which civilization is a thin veneer underneath which human beings can be seen to act on the basis of brutal or irrational drives and instincts. Classicists have quoted Thucydides, psychologists have quoted Freud and Jung, and ethologists have quoted Konrad Lorenz, all of them in a sense providing the same explanation, which was suggested, too, in the Henry James letter quoted in Chapter 1 (p. 3). There is another answer, though, and it is that conduct seemingly civilized and conduct seemingly barbarous both spring from the same set of impulses. They are two sides but of the same coin. The devotion shown to one's own country is usually complemented by the hostility one shows to foreign countries.

It is axiomatic in politics that external threats cause the people of a country to unite. As the French political philosopher Jean Bodin wrote at the beginning of the modern age in Europe: "The best way of preserving a state, and guaranteeing it against sedition, rebellion, and civil war is to keep the subjects in amity one with another, and to this end, to find an enemy against whom they can make common cause."[9]

André Malraux suggested that this disposition might be used in the service of human unity; energies could be united against the forces unleashed by modern technology that have become a common enemy. He visualized it in terms of the battle of Bolgako, in the First World War, where the Germans launched their first poison-gas attack against the Russians. In Malraux's account, after the attack had been launched, German troops spontaneously rushed in to save the Russians who lay dying in the clouds of gas, and both armies of humans joined forces against the inhuman enemy that was the gas.[10] In this moving image, Malraux offered his program for survival.

However, the Germans continued to launch gas attacks against their enemies in the First World War, without again arousing the reaction that Malraux described. More frightful weapons have been used since then, including the atomic bombs dropped by Americans on Japan in 1945, and a world community nonetheless has failed to materialize, although many have argued that the threat to all of us posed by these weapons ought to bring us together.

Natural catastrophes do seem to have a unifying effect on communities, however temporarily; but on the whole, unity in politics seems to be most effectively achieved by a common

[9]Quoted in Waltz, *War*, p. 81.

[10]André Malraux, *Lazarus*, translated by Terence Kilmartin (New York: Grove Press, Inc., 1978).

hostility toward other groups of human beings. The world is unlikely to be united, then, unless we can find a group of creatures from outside the world to unite against.

The Evolutionary Purpose of False Speciation

A clue as to why we failed to unite is provided by a question posed by the British philospher Stuart Hampshire in a recent issue of the *New York Review of Books*, in which he wrote that what should be noted is

> the distinguishing feature of human beings: false speciation, as it is sometimes called—namely, the attachment of normal men through thought and language to the habits, and way of life, of a particular subgroup, accompanied by some measure of hostility or indifference to the habits and ways of life of other subgroups of the same species. That human beings are innately disposed to learn some language, but are not innately disposed to learn one particular language, is a fact about human beings which provokes a question in natural history: what advantage was conferred on the species by the disposition to learn diverse languages and to fall into tightly coherent social groups which are often hostile to one another?
>
> This question may be unanswerable, or unanswerable within the limits of present knowledge. But it is at least evident that this linguistic dispersion of the species is only one part of a deep-seated characteristic of dispersion. . . .[11]

In some ways, this disposition is clearly a disadvantage. Belgium and India are countries, otherwise quite unlike, that provide examples of how difficult it is to maintain national unity when different linguistic groups are hostile to one another. A recent news dispatch from Sudan indicates the immensity of the task of providing a new political structure for a country in which

---

[11]Stuart Hampshire, "The Illusion of Sociobiology," *New York Review of Books,* October 12, 1978, p. 68.

ALEXANDER'S PATH, AND OURS

1,009 languages are spoken.[12] It would be so much easier if everyone spoke the same language, but the failure of Esperanto to be generally adopted provides evidence for the proposition that it runs against the grain to do so.

On the face of it, it would seem that the disposition to be hostile toward members of other groups plays the role of keeping groups apart, and thus of ensuring that human development takes place simultaneously along many diverse lines. That is to humanity's evolutionary advantage, and it may be why the disposition inheres in us. Historically it has been on the basis of experimentation, of advances made by different groups of people, developing differently and often with different intentions, that the human race has developed. The problem is that this behavior pattern, of a diversity guaranteed by a mutual hostility, which has been so useful a tool of human evolution over the course of millions of years, now has become dangerous: the scientific and technical revolutions of modern times have made it so. The question is how such a rooted behavior pattern can be manipulated, moderated, or changed when, as is now the case, a change of circumstances makes it necessary to change behavior.

The Two Ways Out

It is this murky and tangled question that lies at the heart of world politics. If human beings cannot be changed in this respect, and if our political destiny has to be worked out within the confines of a single planet, it seems inevitable that one day the nations will wage a fight to the death, and probably for no very good reason.

That is why the one other alternative is so attractive: to escape from the confines of the world by flying off to colonize the skies. The international problem was made acute, as H. G. Wells wrote, by the abolition of distance; and it can be eased by once again putting distance between us. Only a short time ago, such ideas

---

[12]International *Herald Tribune,* January 3–4, 1981, p. 1.

would have seemed sheer fantasy. With what seriousness they are now taken was made clear at a recent symposium on new research directions organized by the National Aeronautics and Space Administration (NASA) of the United States, at which many of the plans for human habitation in space were discussed.[13] Supporting an expansion of our space programs may well be the most useful practical step that we now can take toward resolution of the ultimate problem of world politics.

This is an approach that is likely to be taken much more seriously if the American space shuttle program proves to be a success. According to a recent report on its progress,

> The shuttle could make going into space so routine that it would become an integral part of life on earth; indeed, if NASA has its way things on earth may never be quite the same again. NASA is much taken with the observation—made by astronauts going to the moon—that the earth is an island in space, and also with the notion that people on islands tend to prosper in proportion to how much they use the sea around them.[14]

While military planners view this shuttle in terms of the military uses of outer space, NASA officials envisage using outer space for science and industry in a major way within a relatively short time. But the creation of self-sustaining human habitations in space, which would separate us from one another in time and distance sufficiently to solve or at least postpone the potentially fatal crisis in international relations, seems likely to take much longer.

The two ultimate solutions—to unify the world, or to escape from it—may be within the realm of our capability, but we do not yet know how to do either one of them, and even if we learn, it is likely to take a long time to do so.

---

[13]The (London) *Times,* January 3, 1981, p. 14.

[14]Henry S. F. Cooper, Jr., "A Reporter At Large: Shuttle-1," *The New Yorker,* February 9, 1981, p. 43.

The importance of what we do in the interim is correspondingly great. To survive and to prosper, we will have to excel in the skills of the very world politics from which we wish to escape. It will benefit us to cultivate those skills.

Holding Opposed Ideas at the Same Time

To know and to act upon the premises of the old-world politics that are still the politics of today result in at least four benefits. It enables us to advance the national interests of the United States by seeing the realities of world politics more clearly. It enables us, by understanding the mainspring of motivation in world politics — self-interest — to construct alliances on a realistic basis to achieve the economic, social, environmental, and political goals that for material or principled reasons we want to advance. Thus Venezuela, oil-rich but cash-poor, invented OPEC in order to lift itself out of poverty, and sought its allies not amongst those who sympathized, but among those whose material interests would be served by the inauguration of such a program. A third benefit, if statesmen can be found to see it, is that the countries that are not actively dissatisfied with their lot in the world have an interest in trying to achieve a resolution of conflicts that threaten to disrupt stability; so that an appeal can be made to foreign governments to act in a constructive manner with respect to issues that do not directly affect them, not out of idealism, but out of far-sighted self-interest. It was in this spirit that Bismarck claimed to act as an "honest broker" at the Congress of Berlin.

Finally there is the balance of power, that inherent disposition in multiple rivalries that tends to keep the rivalries under control. Its mastery is what we must relearn. The skillful construction of new balances could give our own world the decades or centuries of time that are needed to learn whatever is needed to know in order to change the world or to leave it.

The particular danger posed by the idealism that has pervad-

159

ed American and British government, thought, and teaching throughout the century is that it has proceeded from the recognition that we *need* a world order to the delusion that we already *have* one. In doing so, it has neglected the use of the resources, however modest, that are available in the anarchic world of multiple sovereignties—chief among them the balance of power—without gaining anything of value in exchange. This is an unwise approach, and should be abandoned. Above all, until and unless the world changes, we must think about and deal with international politics in their own unique terms; we must not allow ourselves to believe that those terms have changed until the moment that they actually have changed.

One persistent mistake is to think that we already have succeeded in making the escape from the perils that flow from the independence of states. The other mistake is to not realize that someday we have to make it. What is needed is the double vision, and an ability to not confuse the two things that are seen.

As Scott Fitzgerald wrote on the opening page of *The Crack-Up,* "the test of a first-rate intelligence is the ability to hold two opposed ideas in the mind at the same time, and still retain the ability to function." For us it is a test, not merely of our intelligence, but of our ability to survive.

Ever since 1914, the leaders of thought and opinion in the western democracies have seen that the direction of history has to be changed. What has been seen less clearly is that, in the interim, we have to pursue our national interests in a world of nationalisms and power politics. It is not a world in which solutions to problems are readily available. In international relations, problems rarely are solved; at best they are superseded. A successful foreign policy buys time, and, generation after generation, consists of makeshifts and temporizing expedients.

In this short run, which for all we know may last for a considerable length of time, we should endeavor to understand the national aspirations of foreign peoples and the ambitions of their governments; to define our own goals with restraint, with a view

160

towards what is realistically attainable with the resources that we have at hand; and to align our policies with those of foreign governments on the common grounds of moderation and balance.

Out of such endeavors, the more successful European statesmen of the nineteenth century made a certain kind of order in the world. If we could achieve a similar success in the final decades of the turbulent twentieth century, it would be no mean accomplishment.

INDEX

immorality beliefs, 19; and justice, 26; and power, 21, 26, 27; and violence, 28–29
Morgan, Lewis Henry, 123
Morgenthau, Hans, 9, 13, 21, 23, 24, 25, 28, 31, 35, 71, 97, 134, 135
Morgenthau, Henry, 83
Morocco, 96
motivation, personal, 37–38 (see also psychology)
multinational corporations, 142
Murray, Gilbert, 9
Muslim League, 57
Mussolini, Benito, 28, 68, 83

Nansen, F., 48, 51
Nasser, Gamal Abdel, 127
nation, defined, 125
National Aeronautics and Space Administration (NASA), 158
national interest, 27, 38, 114–19
nationalism, 56, 65, 108, 125, 127, 130, 154
Nazis (see Germany, Nazi)
Nigeria, 96
Nixon, Richard, 10, 22, 112
Nobel Prize, 40, 48
No Man's Land, 6; as symbol, 4 (see also First World War)
North Atlantic Treaty Organization (NATO), 119
nuclear weapons, 6, 95
Nuremberg trials, 79–80
Nye, Joseph, 132, 134, 135, 136

oil, 24, 118–19, 133 (see also OPEC)
OPEC, 118, 133, 153, 159 (see also oil)
Open Door policy, 47

Ottoman empire, 45, 46, 56, 58n., 90, 126, 127
Owen, Wilfred, 3
Oxford University, 9

pacifism, 5, 68 (see also war)
Pakistan, 96; and partition, 57; and refugees, 49
Palestine, 126; and partition, 58, 59, 61 (see also Israel)
Papacy, 133
partition, 54–61, 109
passports, 1
patriotism, 154–56
Pearl Harbor attack, 84
Peloponnesian War, 27
Persia (see Iran)
Persians, The (Aeschylus), 99–100
personality and international relations, 35, 36 (see also psychology)
person-state analogy, problems with, 41–61
Peru, 96
petroleum (see oil)
Plato, 14
Poland, 46, 90, 134; and partition, 56, 57; and refugees, 49
political science: behavioral school of, 9, 13; concepts in, 142; model-building in, 135; perspective of, 12–14; scientific method in, 34
Portugal, 96; and partition, 57
power politics, 12–13, 20–25; and democracy, 21–22; forms of power, 24; and independence, 23, 24, 25; and media, 22; and morality, 21, 26, 27; parameters of, 30; and security, 21
president, U.S.: and decision-

168

ABOUT THE AUTHOR

David Fromkin is an international lawyer who divides his time between Europe and the United States. He has served as a foreign policy advisor to presidential candidates in several elections.

Mr. Fromkin writes about government, politics, and foreign policy. His articles have appeared in *Foreign Affairs* and other publications. His book *The Question of Government: An Inquiry into the Breakdown of Modern Political Systems* appeared in 1975.

Mr. Fromkin received a Bachelor of Arts and a Juris Doctor degree from the University of Chicago, and an Academic Postgraduate Diploma in Law from the Institute of Advanced Legal Studies of the University of London.